What Can I Bring?

Sharing Good Tastes and Times in Northern Virginia

A Cookbook by the Junior League of Northern Virginia, Inc.

What Can I Bring?

• *Junior League of Northern Virginia Mission Statement* •

The Junior League of Northern Virginia, Inc. is an organization of women committed to promoting voluntarism, developing the potential of women, and improving the community through the effective action and leadership of trained volunteers. Its purpose is exclusively educational and charitable.

First Printing	April 1999	10,000 copies
Second Printing	July 2000	10,000 copies
Third Printing	March 2003	10,000 copies
Fourth Printing	March 2007	7,500 copies

Photography by Renée Comet

WIMMER
COOKBOOKS

A CONSOLIDATED GRAPHICS COMPANY

800.548.2537   wimmerco.com

Table of Contents

About the Junior League of Northern Virginia, Inc...

The Junior League of Northern Virginia, Inc. is an organization of women committed to promoting voluntarism, developing the potential of women, and improving the community through the effective action and leadership of trained volunteers. Its purpose is exclusively educational and charitable.

Since its founding in 1958 as the Service League of Arlington, the Junior League has been dedicated to making lasting contributions to the lives of Northern Virginia residents. It does this through the involvement of diverse member volunteers and successful partnerships with public, private, governmental, and non-profit agencies. The continual success of the Junior League is due to its unique ability to leverage hundreds of thousands of volunteer hours with the needed financial resources to maximize community impact.

For five decades, the Junior League of Northern Virginia, Inc., has researched and identified the pressing needs of the local community and responded with financial support, new programs and manpower. Throughout the 90's, the organization focused on all aspects of homelessness, including career development for adults, affordable housing for families and educational programs for children in shelters. The signature project of this time was the design, funding and building of a family resource center at a local long-term family shelter. Currently, the Junior League focuses on preparing children for success through a variety of programs including Back-to-School Health Fairs, backpack and school supply distribution project, and programming for children living in area homeless shelters. The current signature project is the development of the Children's Museum of Northern Virginia.

The Junior League of Northern Virginia, Inc. reaches out to women of all races, religions, and national origins who demonstrate an interest in and commitment to volunteerism.

Table of Contents

Appetizers and Beverages 8

Elegant Entrées 48

Soups and Stews 102

One Dish Meals 122

Breads and Brunches 154

Complements 182

Desserts 234

Index 273

Introduction

"What can I bring?" Do these words tumble out of your mouth automatically after "Yes, I'd love to come"? If so, this cookbook is for you. Join the Junior League of Northern Virginia in celebrating good food, great entertaining ideas and the unique pleasures of living in Northern Virginia.

"What Can I Bring?" is a lively assemblage of recipes for your favorite foods. Featured dishes incorporate the best of recent food trends - fresh ingredients and sophisticated, complex flavors from around the world. Many of the recipes are new and innovative, others are 1990s versions of old standbys, and still others are recipes that tie us to our roots. In ease of preparation, they range from quick and easy fixes that can be fit into jam-packed schedules to sophisticated dishes that can highlight special occasions. All have been double- or triple-tested. These are the recipes that we go to time and time again to share with friends, the office or just ourselves. We are honored to share them with you.

The dishes of *"What Can I Bring?"* both reflect and fit our life-styles. Our chosen title reflects one of the biggest challenges we all face - too much to do and not enough time. Our lives are marked by action - fast-paced careers, families, challenging traffic. Hectic life-styles invite innovative solutions, and so, a cooperative spirit has influenced entertaining. If we wait until we can do it all ourselves, it never gets done. It is much better to organize the party and ask for help than to not get together for lack of time to do it properly. Throughout *"What Can I Bring?"* we offer menus and entertaining ideas for many different settings. Nearly all of the recipes are quite portable, so whether you are organizing the event or simply a party-goer bringing a dish, we have a dish to meet your needs.

"What Can I Bring?" also gives you an insider's peek at life here in our corner of the Old Dominion. We think it is a fabulous place to call home, brimming with opportunity and excitement. Located in the shadow of the Nation's Capital and stretching along the banks of the Potomac River, Northern Virginia is a richly diverse region that

What Can I Bring?

stretches from horse country in the foothills of the Blue Ridge Mountains to the placid waters of the tidal Potomac. It bears the physical evidence of defining periods in our nation's history, from the 18th century neighborhoods of Alexandria, George Washington's hometown, to the remains of Civil War forts and battlefields, to the Pentagon, built during World War II. Certainly all the glories of Washington, D.C. lie within minutes of Northern Virginians, but our side of the Potomac, home to well over a million residents, offers enough to keep you exploring and adventuring for years. Look for many ideas for fun events and activities within *our* Northern Virginia neighborhoods, many of which can be transplanted to your neighborhoods, scattered throughout *"What Can I Bring?"*.

"What Can I Bring?" is about individuals, about what each person can bring to the table, to his family, and to his community. When you purchase a copy of this, our first cookbook, you also help the Junior League of Northern Virginia bring trained volunteers, funding and hope to the community of those in need. Through our many programs, we have opened doors when all others were closed, provided opportunity when the future looked bleak, and helped dreams become reality. *"What Can I Bring?"* is one more step in the League's journey. Thanks for your help along the way.

"Don't Miss" Annual Events - Northern Virginia's Best

3rd Monday in February - George Washington Birthday Celebrations - *Tour Mount Vernon for free and take in Alexandria's George Washington Parade, the largest parade in the nation honoring our first five Presidents.*

Monday after Easter - White House Easter Egg Roll - *Technically, not in Northern Virginia, but too good to miss if you have a preschooler.*

Last Week in April - Virginia Historic Garden Week - *Tour stunning homes and gardens in Alexandria, Arlington, Fairfax, and Hunt Country.*

1st Saturday in May - Virginia Gold Cup - *Pack an elegant picnic for this steeplechase classic in The Plains.*

Last Weekend in May - Hunt Country Stable Tour - *Tour premiere thoroughbred racing stables in Loudoun County.*

Early June - Fairfax County Fair - *Savor food, amusements, and entertainment at this huge fair at the Fairfax County Governmental Center.*

Late June - Wolf Trap Jazz and Blues Festival - *Swing with top musical artists at Wolf Trap.*

Last Weekend in July - Virginia Highland Scottish Games - *Don your kilt for this celebration of the clans in Alexandria.*

Late August - Virginia Wine Festival - *Sample Virginia's best at Great Meadow in The Plains.*

Last weekend in September - Occoquan Fall Arts and Crafts Show - *Start your Christmas shopping with a bang in historic Occoquan.*

1st Weekend in October - Waterford Fair - *Celebrate period crafts, music, and historic house tours in the village of Waterford.*

1st Saturday in December - Scottish Walk - *Join the clans in Alexandria for this one-of-a-kind Christmas parade.*

Appetizers and Beverages

Fall Favorites:
Touring, Tasting and Tailgating

Festive Pepper Cheesecake, page 8

Roasted Corn Guacamole, page 34

Virginia Country Ham Spread, page 23

Tantalizing Pea Salad, page 227

Roasted Vegetable Canapés, page 16

Harvest Apple Crisp, page 256

Gingersnaps, page 236

Crispy Caramel Corn, page 272

Hot Ruby Apple Drink, page 45

Harvest Time

Autumn in Northern Virginia. A two-month long string of crisp mornings, warm afternoons, achingly brilliant blue skies and an overwhelming urge to be out of doors, preferably in the country, soaking up all the good weather before winter arrives. The opportunities are endless. The Skyline Drive offers fabulous vistas of fall color, the Shenandoah Valley abounds in crunchy apples and country festivals, steeplechase races draw crowds to the horse country, and football games, whether high school, college or our beloved Redskins, beg for tailgate parties. Perhaps your preferences are for quieter venues, away from the crowds. If so, try a day of wine tastings at regional wineries. Virginia has become one of the largest wine-producing states in the country and many of the wineries are within a two-hour drive of our home base. But don't take our word for it; find out for yourself. Gather some friends together for a day in the country. *"What Can I Bring?"*, they ask. Organize a picnic of hearty finger foods, pack your hampers and head off for a day of delight.

Festive Pepper Cheesecake

1	cup finely crushed tortilla chips
3	tablespoons butter or margarine, melted
2	(8-ounce) packages cream cheese
2	large eggs
2	cups (8 ounces) shredded Monterey Jack cheese with peppers
1	(4.5-ounce) can chopped green chiles
2	cups sour cream
1	cup seeded and chopped yellow and/or red bell pepper
½	cup chopped green onions
⅓	cup chopped tomato
¼	cup chopped pitted ripe olives

- Preheat oven to 350°.
- Combine chips and melted butter; press into the bottom of a 9-inch springform pan.
- Bake at 350° for 15 minutes.
- Beat cream cheese and eggs at medium speed with an electric mixer until smooth; add shredded cheese and green chiles, beating well. Add sour cream, beating well. Pour into prepared crust.
- Bake at 350° for 30 minutes. Let cool on a wire rack. Chill.
- Remove from springform pan to serve. Decorate top with bell pepper and next 3 ingredients.
- Serve with tortilla chips.

Gathering neighbors to celebrate can easily be done by having a progressive dinner or a roaming party. A beginning time is established and a theme is set. You travel as a group from house to house or apartment to apartment. First course is cocktails and appetizers. Second is soup or salad. Next comes the entrée. And finally, scrumptious desserts and coffee.

Elegant Layered Torta

1	cup butter or margarine, cut up and chilled
12	ounces feta cheese, crumbled
1	(8-ounce) package regular or reduced-fat cream cheese
2	garlic cloves, chopped
1	shallot, chopped
½	cup dry vermouth or white wine
½	cup pine nuts, lightly toasted
1	cup sun-dried tomatoes packed in oil, drained and minced
1	cup pesto

- Process first 6 ingredients in a food processor until blended.

- Lightly oil an 8 x 4-inch loaf pan and line with plastic wrap hanging over sides.

- Layer half each of pine nuts, sun dried tomatoes, pesto, and cheese mixture in prepared pan. Repeat layers once. Fold plastic wrap over top, pressing gently until smooth.

- Chill 1 hour or overnight or until firm.

- Unwrap, and invert on a serving platter.

Serves 12 to 14

Unmold on a large platter lined with lettuce leaves or decorative paper. Serve with your favorite crackers or baguette slices. This recipe is a bit time consuming, but it is easy, very elegant, and delicious.

Antipasto Squares

2   (8-ounce) cans refrigerated crescent rolls, divided

¼   pound imported ham, sliced

¼   pound provolone cheese, sliced

¼   pound Genoa salami, sliced

¼   pound Swiss cheese, sliced

¼   pound large pepperoni slices

1   (12-ounce) jar roasted sweet red peppers

3   large eggs

Ground black pepper to taste

3   tablespoons grated Romano cheese

- Spread 1 can crescent roll dough on the bottom of a 9 x 13 x 2-inch pan lightly coated with vegetable cooking spray. Layer ham and next 4 ingredients over dough. Top with red peppers.

- Whisk together eggs, black pepper, and Romano cheese; pour over peppers. Top with remaining can crescent roll dough. Cover with aluminum foil.

- Bake at 350° for 25 minutes. Uncover and bake 10 more minutes or until center is set and top is lightly browned.

- Cut into squares and serve warm or at room temperature.

Serves 4 to 6

*W*rap aluminum foil around cheese to store in the vegetable bin of your refrigerator. It allows the cheese to breathe and is moisture proof.

Puff Pastry Pizza with Onions and Carrots

½ (17¼-ounce) package frozen puff pastry sheets

1 tablespoon butter or margarine

1 tablespoon olive oil

1 medium onion, thinly sliced

3 carrots, thinly sliced

3 tablespoons half-and-half

⅔ cup shredded fontina cheese

½ cup grated Parmigiano-Reggiano cheese

Salt and pepper to taste

¼ cup chopped fresh parsley

- Roll pastry sheet out to a 10 x 15-inch rectangle on a lightly floured surface; fit into a 10 x 15-inch jelly-roll pan. Prick surface with a fork and freeze 2 hours or up to a week.

- Preheat oven to 400°.

- Bake pastry at 400° for 5 minutes. Prick surface again and bake 10 more minutes or until light tan.

- Melt butter and oil in a skillet over medium-high heat; add onion, and cook over high heat, stirring often, until golden. Stir in carrots and cook 3 minutes. Remove from heat and stir in half-and-half. Let cool slightly and stir in half each of fontina and Parmigiano-Reggiano cheeses. Season with salt and pepper.

- Spread vegetable mixture onto prepared crust; top with remaining cheese.

- Bake at 400° for 15 to 20 minutes or until cheese melts (do not brown).

- Sprinkle with parsley. Cut into squares.

Serves 4 as an entrée, 8 as a side dish, or 16 as an appetizer

Crostini with Toppers

⅓ cup olive oil

1 tablespoon minced garlic

2 tablespoons chopped fresh parsley

2 French bread loaves, cut into ½-inch slices

Cheese Topping

Mushroom Topping

Cherry Tomato Topping

- Preheat oven to 350°.

- Combine oil and garlic; stir in parsley. Brush 1 side of each bread slice with garlic mixture and place, brushed side up, on a baking sheet.

- Bake at 350° for 6 to 8 minutes or until lightly toasted. Store in an airtight container up to 2 days.

- Place each topping in an individual serving bowl. Arrange crostini and toppings on a serving platter. Scoop toppings onto crostini.

Serves 8 to 10

Cheese Topping

1 pound mozzarella cheese, cut into 1-inch pieces

1 teaspoon olive oil

½ teaspoon chopped fresh basil

- Combine all ingredients; cover and chill up to 2 days.

(Crostini with Toppers continued)

Mushroom Topping

2	tablespoons butter or margarine
½	cup finely chopped shallots
8	ounces fresh shiitake or wild mushrooms, stemmed and quartered
1	(8-ounce) package fresh white mushrooms, stemmed and quartered
1	teaspoon salt
½	teaspoon freshly ground pepper
½	teaspoon ground thyme
⅓	cup water
2	tablespoons white wine
1½	teaspoons cornstarch

- Melt butter in a skillet over medium-high heat; add shallots and cook until lightly browned. Add shiitake mushrooms and next 4 ingredients. Cover and cook, stirring often, 10 to 12 minutes or until tender.
- Combine ⅓ cup water and wine; whisk in cornstarch. Stir into mushroom mixture and bring to a boil; boil 1 minute. Cover and chill up to 2 days

Cherry Tomato Topping

1	pint cherry tomatoes, quartered
1	tablespoon olive oil
1	teaspoon chopped fresh basil
½	teaspoon lemon juice
½	teaspoon salt
½	teaspoon freshly ground pepper

- Combine all ingredients; cover and chill up to 1 day.

Mushroom Canapés

2 tablespoons butter or margarine, softened
1 dense thin-sliced sandwich bread loaf
4 tablespoons butter or margarine
3 tablespoons finely chopped onion
1 (8-ounce) package fresh mushrooms, finely chopped
2 tablespoons all-purpose flour
1 cup heavy cream
½ teaspoon salt
⅛ teaspoon ground red pepper
1 tablespoon chopped fresh parsley
1½ tablespoons chopped fresh chives
½ teaspoon lemon juice

- Coat bottoms and sides of 24 miniature muffin pan cups with softened butter.

- Cut 1 (3-inch) circle from each bread slice using a round cookie cutter; press bread circles into muffin pan cups, moistening bread with water if too stiff.

- Bake at 400° for 10 minutes or until edges are lightly browned. Let cool on wire racks completely.

- Melt 4 tablespoons butter in a skillet over medium heat; add onion and cook, stirring often, 4 minutes. Add mushrooms and cook, stirring often, 10 to 15 minutes or until moisture has evaporated. Remove from heat.

- Sprinkle flour over mixture and stir well. Stir in cream. Bring mixture to a boil, stirring often, until thickened. Reduce heat and simmer 1 to 2 minutes. Remove from heat; stir in salt and next 4 ingredients.

- Spoon filling into bread shells. Freeze until ready to bake, if desired. Bake frozen canapés on

(Mushroom Canapés continued)

ungreased baking sheets at 350°
for 20 minutes.

- If not freezing, chill filling until
ready to serve. Spoon into shells
just before baking. Bake at 350°
for 10 minutes.

Serves 20 plus

*I*f *the canapés are passed at a cocktail party, a silver platter should not be
used as it will absorb the heat.*

Roasted Vegetable Canapés

1	onion, chopped
4	garlic cloves, minced
¼	cup olive oil
1	medium eggplant, peeled and cut into bite-size pieces
1	cup chopped mushrooms
1	green bell pepper, seeded and chopped
1	red bell pepper, seeded and chopped
1	(8-ounce) can pitted ripe olives, drained and chopped
1	(8-ounce) can tomato sauce
2	tablespoons balsamic vinegar
2	tablespoons light brown sugar
½	teaspoon dried basil, crushed
	Salt and pepper to taste
	Italian bread, cut into thick slices or cubes
	Grated Parmesan cheese (optional)

- Sauté onion and garlic in hot oil in a skillet until tender. Add eggplant and next 5 ingredients. Cover and cook, stirring often, 15 minutes.

- Add vinegar, brown sugar, and basil to vegetable mixture. Reduce heat and simmer, uncovered, 15 minutes or until vegetables are done. Season with salt and pepper. Chill until ready to serve.

- Serve at room temperature with Italian bread and sprinkle with Parmesan cheese, if desired. Or sprinkle with Parmesan cheese and broil until cheese is lightly browned.

Serves 10

Don't have time to slice vegetables for your salad? Stop by the salad bar at your local grocery store. You get what you need and save prep time!

Roasted Red Pepper Dip

2 large red bell peppers or 1 (4-ounce) jar roasted sweet red peppers
4 ounces sun-dried tomatoes packed in oil, drained and patted dry
3 garlic cloves
2 teaspoons ground cumin
2 pickled jalapeño peppers
¼ cup chopped fresh cilantro
2 bunches green onions, white part only coarsely chopped
6 ounces cream cheese, softened
½ teaspoon salt

- Broil fresh bell peppers on a rack in a roasting pan 4 to 6 inches from heat (with electric oven door partially open), turning frequently and watching so flesh does not bruise or burn, until blackened on all sides. Remove from heat and seal in a zip-top plastic bag. Let cool; peel and seed peppers. Or drain store-prepared peppers, pressing between layers of paper towels.

- Process peppers and next 8 ingredients in a food processor until smooth. Season to taste, adding more jalapeño, if desired.

- Serve with blue corn tortilla chips.

Yields 1½ cups

Bell peppers may also be roasted on a wire rack over a medium gas flame on the stove.

When purchasing red bell peppers for this dish, also select a small red, green, and yellow bell pepper for serving the dip. Wash the peppers thoroughly, cut off the tops, remove the cores and seeds, slice the bottoms to allow a firmer "stand," and fill the peppers with the dip. The colors will delight your guests.

Gold Cup Cheese Spread

1	pound shredded sharp cheddar cheese
1	(4½-ounce) can chopped pitted ripe olives
1	(8-ounce) can tomato sauce
1	(4.5-ounce) can chopped green chiles
3	tablespoons cider vinegar
½	cup vegetable oil
2	medium-size sweet onions, chopped
2	garlic cloves, pressed
1	teaspoon Worcestershire sauce
10-12	drops hot sauce
	Salt and pepper to taste
	Sourdough French bread or rolls, cut into ¼-inch-thick slices

- Combine first 11 ingredients; chill at least 1 day.

- Spread cheese mixture on bread slices; cover and chill up to 3 hours, if desired.

- Bake at 350° for 10 minutes or broil until cheese is bubbly.

This cheese spread will keep in the refrigerator for weeks, and it also freezes well.

Sun-Dried Tomato Spread

8   sun-dried tomato halves
    packed in oil, drained
    and patted dry
1   garlic clove, minced
1   tablespoon lemon juice
1   tablespoon chopped
    fresh parsley
1   tablespoon chopped
    fresh basil
4   ounces cream cheese, cut
    up and softened
½   cup sour cream
    Salt and pepper to taste
    Garnish: fresh basil
    sprigs

- Puree first 5 ingredients in a food processor until smooth. Add cream cheese, sour cream, and salt and pepper to taste. Process until smooth, stopping to scrape down sides.

- Transfer spread to a serving bowl and garnish, if desired. Serve with French bread slices.

For a variation add roasted red peppers.

Looking for a different party idea? Try a Reverse Surprise. The guest of honor is already at the site of the party when guests inexplicably arrive to join the gathering, until eventually the guest of honor figures it out.

Hearts of Palm Dip

1   (14-ounce) can hearts of palm, drained and chopped

1   cup (4 ounces) shredded mozzarella cheese

¾   cup light mayonnaise

½   cup grated Parmesan cheese

¼   cup sour cream

2   tablespoons minced green onions

    Paprika to taste

- Combine first 6 ingredients and spoon into a lightly greased 9-inch quiche dish. Sprinkle with paprika to taste.

- Bake at 350° for 20 minutes or until light brown and bubbly. Serve with crackers.

Here are a few ways to help guests distinguish their glasses at a cocktail party. Float different-colored pansies, which are safe to eat, in the glasses and ask guests to remember their colors. Tie different colors of ribbon and numbers of ribbons on the stem of a wineglass. Freeze rose petals in ice cubes (also nice floating in a punch bowl) and use these ice cubes to chill your drinks.

Tomato Company Cups

9	bacon slices, cooked and crumbled
1	large tomato, finely chopped
½	onion, finely chopped
¾	cup (3 ounces) shredded Swiss cheese
½	cup mayonnaise
1	teaspoon dried basil
1	(10-ounce) can refrigerated flaky biscuits

- Preheat oven to 375°.
- Combine first 6 ingredients.
- Separate each biscuit into 2 or 3 thinner ones. Press biscuit pieces into miniature muffin pan cups. Fill biscuit shells evenly with tomato mixture.
- Bake at 375° for 10 to 12 minutes or until bubbly.

Serves 12

For a vegetarian variation, try substituting green bell peppers for bacon, and add a sprinkle of freshly grated Parmesan cheese on top.

Sassy Sausage Dip

1   (16-ounce) package hot or spicy sausage

1   (12- to 14-ounce) can diced salsa-style tomatoes

12-16 ounces cream cheese

Picante sauce to taste

- Brown sausage in a skillet over medium heat, stirring until it crumbles and is no longer pink; drain well.

- Combine sausage, tomatoes, and 12 ounces cream cheese in a microwave-safe bowl. Microwave at HIGH in 4 minute intervals, stirring after each interval, until thoroughly heated. Stir in picante sauce to taste and remaining cream cheese as desired. Serve with chips.

Serves a crowd

Who has the inside ear on what's going on in the world? What's the best source for developing national and international news? Pizza and other carryout establishments near the Pentagon, CIA, and White House report an upsurge in delivery during the days and hours preceding a national or international crisis. Deliveries continue on a 24-hour basis. The pizza of choice? Pepperoni, of course!

Virginia Country Ham Spread

½ cup butter or margarine,
   melted

2 tablespoons poppy
   seeds

2 teaspoons Dijon
   mustard

½ cup finely chopped
   onion

1 teaspoon Worcestershire
   sauce

1 cup (4 ounces) shredded
   Swiss cheese

1 cup (4 ounces) shredded
   cheddar cheese

3 cups cooked country
   ham, ground (about
   1 pound)

3 packages ready-to-serve
   small rolls (20 in each
   package)

• Combine first 8 ingredients,
  stirring well. Spread a large
  amount of ham mixture on each
  roll. Return rolls to foil package.

• Bake at 400° for 10 minutes.

What makes Virginia country ham so distinctive from other hams? It's in the pig's diet. To qualify as the genuine product, pigs destined to grace our tables as country hams are fattened on peanuts.

Hot Reuben Dip

1	(18-ounce) can sauerkraut, rinsed and drained
2	cups (8 ounces) shredded cheddar cheese
2	cups (8 ounces) shredded Swiss cheese
6-8	ounces corned beef, chopped
1	cup mayonnaise

- Pat rinsed and drained sauerkraut dry with paper towels.
- Combine all ingredients, stirring well. Spread into a 9 x 13 x 2-inch pan.
- Bake at 350° for 30 minutes or until hot and bubbly. Serve with cocktail rye bread or baguette slices.

Serves 15 to 20

A big hit at a Super Bowl or sports-oriented party, this dish is best served in its baking dish in the center of a large, flat, towel-lined basket surrounded by breads and crackers. Watch it disappear.

Appetizers

Flank Steak Appetizer

¾ cup soy sauce

4 tablespoons Dijon mustard

1 tablespoon freshly ground black pepper

4-5 garlic cloves, chopped

⅓ cup Worcestershire sauce

1 teaspoon diced fresh ginger

2-2½ pounds flank steak

- In a mixing bowl, whisk first 6 ingredients.

- Combine steak and marinade in a large heavy-duty zip-top plastic bag, turning to coat. Chill 12 hours, turning often. Remove steak from marinade, discarding marinade.

- Grill steak 7 minutes on each side or until done. Remove from heat and let stand at room temperature 8 to 10 minutes.

- Slice thinly on the diagonal. Serve with wooden picks.

Serves 8 to 10

Can be made ahead and served in a fondue pot, a slow cooker, or a heated chafing dish.

Chantilly Crab Dip

½   pound fresh lump or
      canned crabmeat,
      drained

1   (8-ounce) package cream
      cheese

½   cup sour cream

2   tablespoons mayonnaise

1¼   teaspoons
      Worcestershire sauce

½   teaspoon dry mustard

      Pinch of garlic powder

      Pinch of seafood
      seasoning

      Garnishes: paprika,
      chopped fresh parsley

- Combine first 8 ingredients. Spoon into a baking dish.
- Bake at 325° for 30 minutes or until bubbly. Garnish, if desired. Serve with assorted crackers.

Serves 8 to 10

Was a hot dish placed on a wood surface, leaving a milky white heat mark? Immediately upon discovery, generously cover the mark with mayonnaise. Leave until luster is restored to wood.

Crab Melt-a-Ways

1	pound "special" or backfin crabmeat
1	cup butter or margarine
2	(6-ounce) jars sharp cheddar cheese spread
5	tablespoons mayonnaise
1½	teaspoons seasoned salt
1	teaspoon garlic salt
16	English muffins, halved

- Drain and flake crabmeat, removing any bits of shell.

- Beat crabmeat and next 5 ingredients at medium speed with an electric mixer until blended.

- Quarter muffin halves and arrange on a baking sheet. Spread crab mixture generously on muffin quarters; freeze at least 30 minutes.

- Broil frozen melt-a-ways 3 to 5 minutes when ready to serve. Serve hot.

Serves 24

Melt-a-ways can be placed in a heavy-duty zip-top plastic bag after freezing for 30 minutes and kept for up to 6 months. When ready to serve place on a baking sheet and broil 3 to 5 minutes.

These can also be called lifesavers. Prepare ahead and store in the freezer. When company is coming, heat for 10 minutes and serve. Your guests will be amazed.

Lemon-Tuna Mousse

1 (6-ounce) can albacore tuna packed in water, drained

1 tablespoon butter or margarine, softened

1 teaspoon grated lemon rind

2½ tablespoons fresh lemon juice

3 tablespoons extra-virgin olive oil

½ teaspoon dried oregano

2 garlic cloves, chopped

Salt and freshly ground pepper to taste

- Process all ingredients in a food processor until smooth. Chill up to 3 days, if desired.

- Transfer mousse to a serving bowl. Serve at room temperature with crostini, breadsticks, or crisp vegetables.

Serves 4 to 6

Spicy Marinated Shrimp

2 pounds unpeeled, large or jumbo fresh shrimp, peeled and deveined

1½ cups olive oil

½ cup fresh parsley, chopped

4½ teaspoons dried basil

3 teaspoons dried oregano

12 garlic cloves, minced or 4½ teaspoons garlic salt

4½ teaspoons salt (if using garlic salt reduce to 1 teaspoon)

4 tablespoons pepper

4 tablespoons lemon juice

Lettuce leaves

- Peel shrimp and devein, if desired; place shrimp in a shallow dish.

- Combine oil and next 7 ingredients. Reserve ⅓ of marinade for use in basting during cooking. Pour over shrimp, stirring well. Chill at least 1 hour.

- Remove shrimp from marinade; discard used marinade. Put shrimp on skewers and grill over high heat (400° to 425°) or broil, basting with reserved marinade, 3 minutes on each side.

- Serve as an appetizer or a first course on lettuce-lined plates.

Serves 8

*W*hen preparing or serving shrimp or other fragrant "shellfish," use lemon juice on your hands to remove the odor.

If you're serving peel-them-yourself shrimp or crack-them-yourself crabs, your guests will appreciate the small bowls of quartered lemons you've left on the tables and at the sink in the powder room as they clean their hands and get rid of the fishy smells.

Patio Shrimp

¾ cup butter or margarine

1 bay leaf

¼ cup lemon juice

1 garlic clove, crushed

1 teaspoon ground red pepper

¼ cup water

1 pound unpeeled, medium-size fresh shrimp (25 to 30 count)

Freshly ground black pepper

1 baguette, sliced diagonally

- Simmer first 6 ingredients in a saucepan 10 minutes or until butter is melted.

- Peel shrimp and devein, if desired, leaving tails on; place shrimp in a single layer in a baking dish. Pour lemon mixture over shrimp.

- Bake at 350° for 20 to 25 minutes or until shrimp turn pink.

- Remove and discard bay leaf. Sprinkle with freshly ground black pepper and serve immediately with bread to soak up the juices.

Serves 4 to 6

Because shrimp sizes vary greatly, recipes will tell you which is preferred. For example, small shrimp, sweetest and time-consuming to peel, are delicious when used in salads or soups. Medium to large shrimp are generally used with vegetables or pasta dishes. Jumbo to extra-large shrimp are chosen as a finger food with a sauce.

Smoked Salmon Pinwheels

8-10 large flour tortillas

4   (8-ounce) packages
      regular or light
      Boursin cheese

2   hearts of palm, cut into
      eighths

12   ounces smoked salmon,
      thinly sliced

2   commercial roasted
      sweet red peppers,
      drained and cut into
      strips

8   green onions, thinly
      sliced

      Freshly ground black
      pepper

      Fresh dill sprigs

- Place 1 tortilla on a flat surface; spread 1 tablespoon cheese on 1 side of tortilla. Place 1 or 2 strips of hearts of palm at the center of the bottom edge of the tortilla. Place a 3-inch strip of salmon above hearts of palm; add red pepper strips above salmon. Sprinkle green onions over top; season with black pepper to taste.

- Roll tortilla up tightly, beginning at bottom (near hearts of palm). Place seam side down on a plate.

- Repeat procedure with remaining tortillas, cheese, hearts of palm, salmon, red pepper, and green onions.

- Cover with plastic wrap and chill at least 2 hours.

- Cut into ¾-inch slices when ready to serve. Garnish with fresh dill sprigs, if desired.

Gravlax

1	tablespoon sugar
4	tablespoons kosher salt
2	teaspoons white peppercorns, crushed
1	tablespoon cognac (optional)
2½	pounds center cut salmon fillet (2 equal size pieces)
1	bunch fresh dill, chopped

- Combine first 3 ingredients and, if desired, cognac.

- Lay 1 piece of salmon, skin side down, on a large piece of plastic wrap. Moisten with half of sugar mixture; cover with half of chopped dill.

- Repeat procedure with remaining salmon piece, sugar mixture, and dill.

- Sandwich the 2 fillets together and wrap tightly with plastic wrap. Place on a plate and set a 1-pound weight (brick wrapped in plastic wrap or aluminum foil) on top. Chill 24 to 36 hours.

- Scrape off dill mixture using a spoon. Chill salmon until ready to serve, up to 1 week.

- Slice salmon thinly at a 45-degree angle and place on a serving platter.

- Serve with small cooked potatoes or pumpernickel or European rye bread with a bit of mayonnaise and mustard.

Serves 8 to 10

Use only 1 fillet if it is large enough.

Halftime Hot and Spicy Corn Dip

1   (8-ounce) package cream
    cheese
2   tablespoons butter or
    margarine
1   tablespoon garlic salt
2   tablespoons milk
2   tablespoons finely
    chopped jalapeño
    pepper
8   ounces shoepeg corn,
    drained
1   large bag blue corn
    tortilla chips

- Cook first 3 ingredients in a
  saucepan over medium heat until
  creamy and bubbly. Add milk,
  jalapeño, and corn; cook, stirring
  often, until thoroughly heated.
  Spoon into a serving dish.

- Serve with blue corn tortilla chips.

Serves 8 to 10

Fill a large stainless steel bowl with loosely packed CLEAN snow. Staying outside, add cold milk, vanilla, and sugar to taste, stirring quickly and gently. Wonder of winter! Snow cream!

Roasted Corn Guacamole

2 cups frozen corn kernels
2 tablespoons olive oil
Juice of 1 lime
2 tablespoons salsa
1 cup fresh or commercial avocado, pureed
1 teaspoon ground cumin

- Combine corn and oil in an ovenproof baking dish, stirring to coat.
- Broil 10 to 12 minutes, stirring occasionally, until corn is roasted. Let cool completely.
- Combine lime juice and next 3 ingredients, stirring well. Stir in cooled corn. Chill 4 to 6 hours.
- Serve with tortilla chips.

Serves 10 to 12

Pay attention when you are roasting the corn; otherwise, it will pop and stick to the inside of your oven.

Place plastic wrap on the surface of the guacamole when storing in the refrigerator. Oxygen causes avocado to turn brown.

Black Bean Salsa

2   (15-ounce) cans black
     beans, drained
1   (17-ounce) can reduced-
     sodium, whole kernel
     corn, drained
2   large tomatoes, seeded
     and chopped
½-1 purple onion, chopped
¼   cup fresh cilantro,
     chopped
¼   cup lime juice
2   tablespoons olive oil
2   tablespoons red wine
     vinegar
¼   teaspoon ground red
     pepper
     Salt and pepper to taste
1   large avocado, peeled
     and chopped
     Garnishes: avocado
     slices, fresh parsley
     sprigs

• Combine first 10 ingredients,
  stirring well. Chill until ready to
  serve.
• Stir in avocado when ready to
  serve. Garnish, if desired. Serve
  with tortilla chips or as a side
  dish.

Serves 6 as a side dish,
10 to 12 as an appetizer

*To ripen avocado, put in a paper sack with a ripe apple. Poke small holes in
the paper sack so the carbon dioxide can escape.*

Black Bean Hummus

1 (15- to 16-ounce) can
garbanzo beans,
drained reserving
liquid

⅓ cup tahini

⅓ cup lime juice

2 garlic cloves, chopped

1 (15-ounce) can black
beans, drained

Ground red pepper to
taste

Salt and ground black
pepper to taste

Pita bread, cut into
triangles

Garnish: ⅓ cup chopped
fresh parsley or
parsley sprigs

- Rinse garbanzo beans and drain well. Puree garbanzo beans and next 3 ingredients in a food processor until smooth. Spoon into a bowl.

- Process black beans in food processor until coarsely chopped; add to garbanzo mixture. Stir in enough garbanzo liquid until the consistency of thick mayonnaise. Add red pepper, salt, and black pepper to taste.

- Transfer to a serving bowl; garnish, if desired.

Serves 15 to 20

Rubbing parsley on your hands will get rid of garlic smell.

Black-Eyed Pea Dip

4	(16-ounce) cans black-eyed peas, cooked and drained
5	pickled jalapeño peppers, finely chopped
1	tablespoon pickled jalapeño juice
1	tablespoon finely chopped onion
1	(4-ounce) can green chiles, chopped
1	garlic clove, minced or 1 teaspoon garlic powder
1	teaspoon chili powder
2	cups (8 ounces) shredded sharp cheddar cheese
¼	pound butter or margarine
	Shredded sharp cheddar cheese (optional)

- Process first 7 ingredients in a blender until smooth.

- Microwave cheese and butter at MEDIUM (50% power), stirring often, until melted; stir into black-eyed pea mixture.

- Pour dip into a chafing dish. Serve hot with corn chips. Sprinkle with extra cheese, if desired.

Serves 16 to 20

You may also melt cheese and butter in the top of a double boiler over boiling water, stirring constantly.

*O*n New Year's Day, at least a spoonful of black-eyed peas is a must in most traditional Southern homes. Legend says that by eating black-eyed peas, one will have good luck for the year.

Kingstowne Wraps

1½ cups shredded cole slaw mix

½ cup water chestnuts, finely chopped

¼ cup thinly sliced green onions

2 teaspoons sesame oil

4 tablespoons plum sauce, divided

4-6 flour tortillas

- Combine first 4 ingredients and 3 tablespoons plum sauce, mixing well.

- Spread remaining 1 tablespoon plum sauce evenly over tortillas; spread ½ cup cole slaw mix on each tortilla to within ¼ inch of edges. Roll tortillas up tightly and wrap in plastic wrap. Chill at least 1 hour.

- Cut diagonally into 1-inch slices when ready to serve.

Yields 2 dozen

When hosting a gathering, set out serving pieces ahead of time with slips of paper labeling the dish. This way if someone arrives early and wants to assist you it is easy.

Chutney Cheese Ball

12 ounces cream cheese

1 bunch green onions, chopped

1 small box raisins

9 bacon slices, cooked and crumbled

2 tablespoons sour cream

1 teaspoon curry powder

1 small package chopped peanuts

1 jar chutney

Flaked coconut

• Combine first 7 ingredients and half of chutney; form into a ball. Cover ball with remaining half of chutney and sprinkle with coconut.

Serves 12 to 16

Parmesan-Herb Almonds

¾ cup grated Parmesan cheese

1½ tablespoons dried Italian seasoning

2¼ teaspoons garlic powder

½ teaspoon paprika

2 egg whites

2 cups whole natural almonds

- Preheat oven to 325°.
- Combine first 4 ingredients.
- Whisk egg whites until opaque in color and soft peaks form; add almonds, tossing to coat. Add cheese mixture, tossing gently to coat. Arrange almonds on a single layer on a lightly greased baking sheet.
- Bake at 325° for 15 minutes. Gently toss almonds and arrange again in a single layer. Bake 15 more minutes. Toss gently.
- Turn oven off and leave almonds in oven with door ajar 20 minutes.
- Remove from oven and cool completely. Store in an airtight container up to 1 week.

Serves 8

We always need hostess gifts and remembrances for teachers, bus drivers, baby sitters, and other important people in our lives. These almonds can be packaged in assorted pretty containers you buy or create yourself. Be sure to include a copy of the recipe.

Party Pecans

½ cup butter or margarine

2 egg whites

1 cup sugar

1 pound shelled pecan halves

- Melt butter on a baking sheet and spread to coat.

- Beat egg whites at medium speed with an electric mixer until soft peaks form; gradually beat in sugar at high speed until stiff peaks form. Gradually stir in pecans until all are coated. Spread over buttered baking sheet.

- Bake at 300° for 30 minutes, stirring every 10 minutes.

Serves 20 plus

These are great for gift giving. During the year, enjoy the adventure of searching for unusual ways to package them. For the fisherman, place in small sealed bags in a tackle box. For the home improvement sort, place in a toolbox. The gardener will enjoy them in a clay or decorative flower pot. The teacher will appreciate the thoughtfulness with pencils or a gift certificate attached with ribbon. The containers are as limitless as your imagination.

Bride's Punch

1 (12-ounce) can frozen orange juice concentrate, thawed and undiluted

1 (12-ounce) can frozen lemonade concentrate, thawed and undiluted

1 (46-ounce) can pineapple juice

2½ quarts water

28 ounces ginger ale

1 (6-ounce) jar maraschino cherries

• Combine first 4 ingredients, stirring well. Stir in ginger ale and cherries when ready to serve.

Serves 32

*T*hinking *of creative ways to serve punch. Try using a new large plastic garden pot liner placed inside a large clay pot or basket. This would work for an outdoor party or a garden-theme bulb exchange party.*

Celebration Mint Tea

3	cups boiling water
4	regular-size tea bags
9-10	fresh mint sprigs
¾	cup sugar
¼	cup fresh lemon juice
1	cup orange juice
4	cups water

- Pour 3 cups boiling water over tea bags and mint. Cover and steep 5 minutes.
- Remove tea bags and mint, squeezing bags gently. Stir in sugar and next 3 ingredients. Serve over ice. Garnish, if desired.

Yields 2 quarts

Make double since this will go fast!

Holiday Irish Coffee Eggnog

1	quart commercial eggnog
1¼	cups hot brewed coffee
⅔	cup Irish cream liqueur
½	cup brandy
½	cup sugar

- Combine all ingredients, stirring to dissolve sugar. Chill overnight.

Serves 4

For a colorful flair, dust the tops of your cups of eggnog with powdered cocoa, colored sugars, chocolate shavings, or a complement of your choice.

Holiday Cider

1	quart apple cider
4	whole cloves
4	whole allspice
3	cinnamon sticks
1	ounce brandy

- Bring cider almost to a boil in a saucepan.

- Place spices on a square of cheese-cloth and tie up with a string; add spice bag to cider and simmer 30 minutes. Remove spice bag and bring cider almost to a boil.

- Serve cider in cups and float a small amount of brandy on top of each serving.

Serves 4

How can you always have ice on hand for a party? Frequently empty your ice cube trays or automatic ice maker into large zip-top plastic bags and freeze. When it is time to entertain, you are ready and no one has to buy or bring ice. Caution: Do not store the ice in brown paper sacks. If the power goes out for an extended period of time you will have a mess.

Hot Ruby Apple Drink

46	ounces apple juice
6	ounces frozen lemonade concentrate, thawed and undiluted
1	(14-ounce) jar spiced apple rings, undrained
2	tablespoons butter or margarine
2	cinnamon sticks

• Cook all ingredients in a large Dutch oven over medium heat until thoroughly heated. Do not boil. Reduce heat and simmer 1 to 2 hours.

Serves 8 to 10

*H*osting a winter holiday open house, snowed in and neighbors might be dropping by to warm up, or just in need of that childhood memory of the way the house smells during the holiday, then you need to let this warm drink simmer on the stove all day. Have your glassware handy and ready to serve. You will be creating new memories for others.

Coffee Liqueur Smoothie

1   ounce Kahlúa

1   ounce rum

2   large scoops vanilla ice
     cream

2   large or 4 small ice cubes

- Process all ingredients in a
  blender until smooth and thick.
  Serve immediately in a tall wineglass.

Serves 1

This "adult milk shake" can be served any time of the year. Whether you're sitting by the fireside, watching the surf at the beach, or just relaxing on the screened porch watching the leaves change, serve in a wineglass and enjoy good conversation.

Elegant
Entrées

Guaranteed to Impress the Neighbors

Cream of Carrot and
Lemon Soup, *page 104*

Stuffed Flank Steak, *page 48*

Portobello Mushroom Risotto
with Feta Cheese, *page 206*

Walnut Broccoli, *page 183*

Endive with Hot Bacon Dressing, *page 230*

Frozen Lime Torte
with Blackberry Sauce and
Fresh Fruit, *page 246*

Getting To Know You

You're new in town. How do you find your niche in this richly diverse and geographically complex region we call Northern Virginia? The military community, which is well represented in our area, relies on a lovely institution known as a Hail and Farewell to welcome newcomers and bid adieu to those leaving town. Most career military officers and their families call Northern Virginia home at least once during their service lives, since a tour of duty at the Pentagon, the military headquarters located in our midsts on the banks of the Potomac, is practically de rigueur. And of course, transience is not unique to the military. Politicians and civil servants, corporate types, high tech hot shots, people of all professions are constantly coming and going in Northern Virginia.

So the next time you connect with a newcomer, whether it's the new family moving in down the street or an old college chum relocating to town, gather your crowd together for an evening of fun and introductions. Reward your local friends by tackling the menu yourself, but when they ask, *"What Can I Bring?,"* task each to bring a "five favorites" list of restaurants or biking trails or kids' outings or other common denominators. Your old friends will enjoy your efforts, and the newcomers will suddenly feel more at home armed with their "old-timers'" secrets!

Stuffed Flank Steak

2 pounds flank steak, trimmed
¼ teaspoon paprika
1 teaspoon salt
¼ teaspoon pepper
¼ teaspoon mustard
¼ teaspoon ground ginger
1 teaspoon Worcestershire sauce
¼ cup butter or margarine
2 tablespoons chopped onion
1 cup breadcrumbs
¼ teaspoon salt
2 tablespoons chopped parsley
3 tablespoons chopped celery
1 large egg, lightly beaten
   Vegetable oil
2 tablespoons all-purpose flour
1 cup water or stock
1 cup red wine

- Combine paprika and next 5 ingredients. Coat steak with dry mixture

- Melt butter in a skillet over medium heat; add onion and sauté until tender. Add breadcrumbs and next 4 ingredients to onion, stirring well. Spread mixture over steak; roll loosely and tie with string.

- Sear steak on all sides in hot oil in a skillet. Transfer to a baking dish, reserving oil in skillet.

- Add flour, 1 cup water or broth, and wine to oil in skillet, stirring until smooth. Pour mixture over steak.

- Bake steak, covered, at 325° for 1½ hours.

Serves 4

Beef Burgundy

2½	pounds beef, cubed
½	cup all-purpose flour
3	tablespoons oil
2	garlic cloves, finely chopped
2	cups dry red wine
	Hot water
3	bay leaves
1½	teaspoons salt
4	tablespoons fresh parsley
6	bacon slices, diced
1	cup chopped onion
1½	cups sliced mushrooms
	Pepper to taste

- Dredge beef cubes in flour. Brown in hot oil in a skillet over medium heat. Add garlic and sauté 1 minute. Transfer to a 2-quart baking dish. Add wine and hot water to barely cover meat. Add bay leaves, salt, and parsley.
- Bake, covered, at 325° for 2 hours.
- Fry bacon in skillet; add onion and cook 3 minutes. Add mushrooms and cook until bacon is crisp; drain fat.
- Remove casserole from oven. Drain fat; remove and discard parsley and bay leaves. Add onion mixture and pepper to casserole; bake, covered, 30 more minutes or until meat is tender.

Serves 6 to 8

*H*olidays are meant to be shared. Enjoy your gathering this year with the Menorah and Christmas tree. It is a way to learn about both heritages and traditions. Invite each guest to bring a favorite holiday food and tell the memory of how this became a favorite. Stories from childhood often unite a group, leaving a warm feeling to send home with your guests.

Barbecued Short Ribs

¼ cup chopped onion

4 tablespoons sugar

⅛ teaspoon pepper

3 tablespoons vinegar

¼ cup ketchup

Favorite choice of commercial barbecue sauce

6 medium beef short ribs

- Combine first 5 ingredients; add an equal amount of commercial barbecue sauce to double the amount, stirring well.

- Arrange ribs, meat side down and edges just touching, in a 9 x 13 x 2-inch baking dish. Pour sauce over ribs, saturating ribs.

- Bake at 400° for 1½ hours. Reduce oven temperature to 325°; bake 45 to 60 minutes or until meat is tender.

Serves 3

When setting your table for this dish, use two coordinating colors of cloth napkins: one for the lap and the other for your hands. Different color bandannas make colorful napkins for an outdoor gathering. Tie them around each set of utensils. After the event, they all go in the washing machine.

Beef Godunov

2   teaspoons butter or margarine

3   pounds top sirloin, cut into 2-inch-long ¼-inch-thick strips

3   large onions, chopped

1½ cups sliced fresh or 2 cups canned mushrooms

1   cup beef broth

1   (12-ounce) can tomato sauce

2   bay leaves

1   tablespoon salt

⅛   teaspoon pepper

1   tablespoon Worcestershire sauce

1   cup sherry

3   cups sour cream

    Hot cooked noodles or rice

- Melt butter in a Dutch oven over medium heat; cook sirloin strips and onion in batches until meat is browned. Add mushrooms and sauté until tender.

- Simmer steak, onion, mushrooms, broth, and next 5 ingredients, covered, in Dutch oven 1 hour. Cool.

- Gradually stir in sherry. Cook 30 minutes. Cool. Cook until thoroughly heated. Stir in sour cream (do not boil). Remove and discard bay leaves. Serve on noodles or rice.

Serves 4 to 6

For an easy fall centerpiece, collect several colorful leaves from outside. Rinse leaves to make certain they are clean and suitable for your table. Once rinsed, dry carefully with a paper towel. Arrange in a circle with the stems facing the interior for candlesticks, pumpkins, gourds, harvest corn, or mums. Layer the leaves slightly so there will be continuous color underneath your arrangement. Bringing the outdoors in is always a way to salute Mother Nature.

Tailgate Brisket

1   large beef brisket,
       trimmed

1-2 teaspoons Liquid Smoke

1   tablespoon celery seed
       (or to taste)

1   teaspoon garlic salt (or
       to taste)

     B-B-Q Sauce, recipe
     follows

- Prick brisket with a fork all over. Rub with Liquid Smoke, celery seed, and garlic salt.

- Bake, covered, at 250° for 5 to 6 hours or until tender.

- Slice and serve with B-B-Q Sauce. (Cooking the meat long and slow makes it tender. Leftovers are great for sandwiches with a little meat juice on bread.)

Brisket is often served at large gatherings or outdoor events. It can be served with buns, bread, cornbread, beans, slaw, potatoes, corn on the cob, or just in slices with our tasty B-B-Q Sauce.

B-B-Q Sauce

1   (14-ounce) bottle
    ketchup

3   tablespoons butter or
    margarine

3   tablespoons brown
    sugar

2   tablespoons Liquid
    Smoke

4   tablespoons
    Worcestershire sauce

3   teaspoons dry mustard

2   teaspoons celery seed

¼   teaspoon ground red
    pepper

½   cup water

    Salt and ground black
    pepper to taste

- Cook all ingredients over medium heat 10 minutes, stirring occasionally.

- Separate a small amount with which to "paint" uncooked meat before barbecuing. Serve remainder warm.

Serves 6 to 8

This tasty sauce will keep in your refrigerator for weeks. Enjoy it as a complement to Tailgate Brisket.

Marinated Beef Tenderloin

1½ cups ketchup

3 teaspoons prepared mustard

¾ teaspoon Worcestershire sauce

2¼ cups water

3 (0.7-ounce) envelopes Italian dressing mix

1 (4- to 6-pound) beef tenderloin, trimmed

Garnishes: watercress, red and green grapes

- Combine first 5 ingredients, mixing well. Reserve ⅓ of marinade to use for basting.

- Spear beef in several places and place in a heavy-duty zip-top plastic bag.

- Add marinade to bag and seal tightly. Place in a shallow pan in the refrigerator 5 hours, turning occasionally.

- Drain tenderloin, discarding marinade. Place tenderloin on a rack in a roasting pan. Bake at 425° for 30 to 45 minutes or until a meat thermometer inserted into thickest portion registers 150° for medium rare or 160° for medium, basting occasionally with reserved marinade.

- Transfer tenderloin to a serving platter. Garnish, if desired.

Grilled Flank Steak

½   cup soy sauce

⅜   cup vegetable or garlic oil

1½   tablespoons Oriental sesame oil

3   garlic cloves, minced

3   tablespoons minced fresh ginger

6   green onions, white and green parts trimmed and minced

1   (2- to 2½-pound) flank steak

     Salt and freshly ground pepper to taste

- Process first 6 ingredients in a blender 1 to 2 minutes. Reserve ⅓ of marinade to use for basting.

- Rub steak with salt and pepper.

- Combine steak and marinade in a shallow dish or a large zip-top plastic bag. Let stand at room temperature 2 hours, or cover, seal, and chill overnight. Remove steak from marinade, discarding marinade.

- Grill steak 4 to 5 inches above hot coals 5 minutes on each side (for rare meat), basting occasionally with reserved marinade. (Steak may also be broiled, if desired.) Discard remaining marinade.

Serves 4 to 6

Always bring meat and fish to be grilled to room temperature before cooking. This reduces cooking time and ensures more even cooking.

Pollo Saltimbocca

4   skinned and boned chicken breasts

Salt to taste

4   teaspoons chopped fresh sage

4   thin slices prosciutto

½   cup all-purpose flour

½   cup olive oil

½   cup white cooking wine

2   tablespoons capers

1   cup marinated artichoke hearts, quartered

3   tablespoons butter or margarine

- Sprinkle chicken lightly with salt; coat evenly with sage. Place 1 prosciutto slice on each chicken breast and flatten chicken to ⅜-inch thickness using a meat mallet or rolling pin. Lightly flour chicken-prosciutto stacks.

- Cook in hot oil in a skillet, prosciutto side down, until done, turning once. Transfer to a serving platter. Wipe skillet clean.

- Cook wine and capers in skillet until wine is reduced by one-half. Add artichokes and butter; pour sauce over chicken.

Serves 4

*W*hen responding to the invitation, people often ask "What can I bring?" It is up to the hostess and the chosen menu to give the guest an option, whether it is a green salad, a bottle of wine, or dessert.

Roast Chicken with Orange-Port Sauce

1	large roasting chicken
1	tablespoon butter or margarine, softened
1	teaspoon Dijon mustard
1	teaspoon soy sauce
2	tablespoons Port, divided
½	cup orange marmalade
2	teaspoons cornstarch
¾	cup water
	Salt and pepper to taste

- Preheat oven to 300°.
- Remove giblets from chicken, reserving for another use. Rinse chicken well inside and out with cold water; pat dry.
- Rub chicken well with butter and place in a roasting pan.
- Bake at 300° for 2½ hours or until tender.
- Bring mustard, soy sauce, 1 tablespoon Port, and marmalade to a boil in a small saucepan. Reduce heat and simmer 10 minutes, stirring occasionally.
- Remove chicken from oven and brush lavishly with glaze. Bake 30 more minutes or until golden.
- Transfer chicken to a serving platter, reserving drippings in pan. Add remaining 1 tablespoon Port to drippings and cook over medium-high heat, stirring to loosen browned particles.
- Combine cornstarch and ¾ cup water, stirring until smooth; add to Port mixture, stirring until smooth. Season with salt and pepper.
- Serve sauce over sliced chicken or as a side dish at the table.

Serves 6 to 8

Store candles in the refrigerator and they will burn longer and slower.

Sherried Artichoke Chicken

12   skinned and boned chicken breast halves

    Paprika to taste

    Salt and pepper to taste

½   cup butter or margarine, divided

2   (15-ounce) cans artichoke hearts, drained and quartered

1   pound fresh mushrooms, sliced

½   teaspoon dried tarragon

2   rounded teaspoons all-purpose flour

2   cups chicken broth

1   cup sherry

- Season chicken with paprika, salt, and pepper.
- Melt 4 tablespoons butter in a skillet over medium heat. Add chicken and sauté until browned. Combine chicken and artichoke hearts in a 9 x 13 x 2-inch baking dish.
- Melt remaining 4 tablespoons butter in skillet; add mushrooms and tarragon. Sauté 5 minutes. Sprinkle flour over mushrooms; gradually add sherry and broth, stirring until blended. Simmer 5 minutes or until sauce is thickened.
- Pour mixture over chicken and artichokes.
- Bake, covered, at 350° for 45 minutes, adding additional broth as needed to keep chicken moist.

Serves 8 to 10

*W*hether entertaining at home or for the neighborhood block party, arranging the table and food are important. For a buffet table, stack plates at the beginning and napkins, utensils, and beverages at the other end. Also, having a separate area for beverages and desserts will free up the space and help the flow of people.

Spicy Chicken with Peanut Sauce

2	packages spicy Thai peanut sauce mix
2	(10-ounce) cans coconut milk
4	skinless chicken breasts
4	cups white Thai rice, cooked
4	green onions, chopped

- Preheat oven to 350°.
- Cook peanut sauce according to package directions using coconut milk.
- Combine chicken and peanut sauce in an 8-inch-square baking dish.
- Bake at 350° for 30 minutes.
- Spoon hot cooked rice onto a serving platter. Spoon chicken and sauce over rice. Sprinkle with green onions and serve immediately.

Serves 4 to 6

Try this variation on this dish. Poach cubed chicken breasts, skewer with choice of vegetables, and pour peanut sauce over to serve as an appetizer or fun party dish. Keep warm in oven until ready to serve.

Cumin Chicken with Hot Citrus Salsa

2 cups chopped tomato

2 medium oranges, chopped with juice reserved

1½ tablespoons chopped fresh cilantro or parsley

2 teaspoons grated fresh ginger

1 small jalapeño pepper, finely chopped

4 skinned and boned chicken breasts

1½ teaspoons ground cumin

¼ teaspoon salt

¼ teaspoon pepper

1 tablespoon vegetable oil

Hot cooked rice

- Combine first 5 ingredients and set aside.

- Place chicken between 2 sheets of plastic wrap and flatten to ¼-inch thickness using a meat mallet or rolling pin.

- Combine cumin, salt, and pepper; rub mixture on both sides of chicken.

- Cook chicken in hot oil in a skillet over medium heat 4 minutes on each side or until done.

- Top chicken with salsa and serve with hot cooked rice.

Serves 4

When entertaining friends or business associates, remember to remain confident and comfortable. If the host and hostess are calm and comfortable, everyone else will be relaxed and having the time of their lives.

Plum Chicken with Snow Peas

3	pounds skinned and boned chicken pieces
2	tablespoons vegetable oil
½	cup chopped onion
1	garlic clove, minced
1½	teaspoons chopped fresh ginger
⅓	cup plum sauce (found in Oriental section of most grocery stores)
¼	cup frozen lemonade concentrate
¼	cup chili sauce
2	tablespoons soy sauce
1½	tablespoons lemon juice
1	teaspoon dry mustard
1½	cups snow peas
3	cups water
3	cups cooked rice

- Brown chicken in hot oil in a skillet 4 minutes on each side. Transfer chicken to a 9 x 13 x 2-inch baking dish, reserving 1 tablespoon drippings in skillet.

- Add onion, garlic, and ginger to drippings and sauté until tender.

- Combine plum sauce and next 5 ingredients; stir into onion mixture and bring to a boil. Cover, reduce heat, and simmer 5 minutes. Spoon mixture over chicken.

- Bake at 350° for 45 minutes or until done, basting with drippings occasionally.

- Bring 3 cups water to a boil in a saucepan; add snow peas and boil 2 minutes. Drain and rinse with cold water.

- Serve chicken over hot cooked rice and top with snow peas.

Serves 6

It seems as if people are always in motion, so making it easy to RSVP to your gathering should be a priority if possible. List as many numbers as you are comfortable: home, work, mobile telephone, fax, and E-mail address. You are more likely to hear from people and less likely to have to make follow up telephone calls.

Lite and Spicy Peanut and Chicken Pasta

⅓ cup lite crunchy peanut butter

¼ teaspoon coconut extract

1¼ cups reduced-fat chicken broth

½ teaspoon crushed red pepper

2 garlic cloves, minced

1 teaspoon grated fresh ginger

2 tablespoons lite soy sauce

½ teaspoon hot pepper sauce

2 teaspoons sugar

Salt and pepper to taste

2 cups cubed chicken

1 tablespoon cornstarch

2 tablespoons water

6 cups noodles, cooked

Garnish: chopped green onions

- Cook first 10 ingredients in a medium saucepan over medium heat 10 to 15 minutes.

- Broil chicken until done.

- Combine cornstarch and 2 tablespoons water, stirring until smooth; add to sauce and cook 1 minute or until thickened.

- Combine chicken, sauce, and hot cooked noodles, tossing to coat. Garnish, if desired.

Serves 6

Marinate chicken breasts in the sauce and grill for a good sandwich. Or combine chopped cooked chicken and sauce for a delicious cold chicken salad.

Chicken with Fruit Salsa

6   chicken breasts
    Teriyaki sauce
½   mango, peeled and
    chopped
2   kiwi, peeled and
    chopped
1   peach, peeled and
    chopped
½   red bell pepper, seeded
    and chopped
1   small purple onion,
    chopped
⅛   cup minced fresh
    cilantro

• Combine chicken breasts and
  teriyaki sauce to cover in a large,
  shallow dish; chill several hours
  or overnight.

• Grill chicken over medium heat
  (300° to 350°) until thoroughly
  done.

• Combine mango and next 5
  ingredients in a small bowl. Serve
  fruit salsa over chicken.

Serves 6

*Not sure whether your peaches, pineapples, pears, or other fruits are ripe?
Give them a sniff. If they smell good, they're ripe.*

Chicken Tetrazzini

¼ cup butter or margarine, melted

¼ cup all-purpose flour

1 cup chicken broth

1 cup whipping cream

2 tablespoons sherry

Salt and pepper to taste

2 cups cubed chicken

1 cup sliced fresh mushrooms

7 ounces spaghetti, cooked

½ cup grated Parmesan cheese

- Cook butter and flour to make a roux; add broth and next 3 ingredients. Bring to a boil and boil 1 minute.

- Add chicken, mushrooms, and spaghetti, stirring well.

- Transfer to a 9 x 13 x 2-inch baking dish. Sprinkle evenly with Parmesan cheese. Chill overnight.

- Bake at 350° for 30 minutes.

Serves 6

To make a white roux, blend flour and butter in a saucepan and cook until foamy. Do not brown.

Chicken Breasts Lombardy

6   skinned and boned
    chicken breasts
    Salt and pepper to taste
½   cup all-purpose flour
1¼ cups butter or olive oil,
    divided
¾   cup Marsala wine
½   cup chicken stock
½   cup sliced mushrooms
½   cup grated Parmesan
    cheese
½   cup (2 ounces) shredded
    mozzarella cheese

- Place chicken between 2 sheets of plastic wrap and flatten to ⅛-inch-thickness using a meat mallet or rolling pin. Salt and pepper to taste and dredge in flour.

- Melt 1 cup butter in a skillet over medium heat; add chicken and sauté 3 to 4 minutes on each side or until lightly browned. Transfer to a greased 9 x 13 x 2-inch baking dish, reserving drippings in skillet.

- Add wine and chicken stock to drippings, stirring to loosen browned particles; simmer 10 minutes.

- Melt remaining ¼ cup butter in a separate skillet over medium heat; add mushrooms and sauté until tender. Spoon mushrooms over chicken.

- Combine cheeses and sprinkle over mushrooms; pour sauce over top.

- Bake at 400° for 10 to 12 minutes. Broil 1 to 2 minutes.

Serves 4 to 6

If you regularly keep a full freezer, you need to know when there's been a power failure. Wash an empty half-gallon milk jug, fill halfway up with water, and freeze. Once frozen, place the jug on its side in the freezer. If you ever lose power for an extended time while you're away from your home, you'll know when you return because the ice in the jug will have melted and refrozen in the opposite "direction."

Marinated Chicken Breasts

¾ cup firmly packed brown sugar

½ cup olive oil

½ cup apple cider vinegar

4½ garlic cloves, crushed

4½ tablespoons Dijon mustard

4½ tablespoons lemon juice

2¼ teaspoons salt

½ teaspoon pepper

8 chicken breast halves

- Combine first 8 ingredients, stirring well.

- Place chicken in a heavy-duty zip-top plastic bag; pour liquid into bag. Seal and shake well. Chill up to 30 hours.

- Grill chicken over hot coals 8 minutes on each side.

Serves 8

Turn grilled chicken and other meats with tongs rather than with a fork. Forks pierce the meat, allowing juices to escape.

Chicken Marsala

2   tablespoons butter or margarine

4   skinned and boned chicken breasts

1   (10¾-ounce) can cream of mushroom soup, undiluted

⅓   cup sour cream

⅓   cup water

2   tablespoons Marsala wine

1   tablespoon minced garlic

1   teaspoon paprika

¼   teaspoon ground white pepper

⅛   teaspoon poultry seasoning

Hot cooked rice

- Melt butter in a skillet over medium heat; add chicken and cook until done. Transfer chicken to a serving platter, reserving drippings in skillet.

- Add soup and next 7 ingredients to drippings. Cook, stirring occasionally, until thoroughly heated.

- Serve chicken over hot cooked rice and top with sauce.

Serves 4

Pesto Grilled Chicken

8   skinned and boned
    chicken breast halves
1   cup balsamic vinegar
⅔   cup olive oil
4   garlic cloves, crushed
    Salt and pepper to taste
1   large tomato
    Commercial pesto sauce
½   cup pine nuts
½   cup grated fontina or
    mozzarella cheese
⅓   cup thinly sliced ham

- Place chicken in a shallow pan. Combine first 4 ingredients and pour half of mixture over chicken. Chill at least 1 hour.

- Slice tomato and place in a shallow dish; pour remaining half of dressing over top. Chill at least 1 hour.

- Drain tomato and chop.

- Grill chicken 4 to 5 minutes on each side, brushing often with pesto. Transfer chicken to a serving platter.

- Brush additional pesto over chicken; top with chopped tomato, pine nuts, cheese, and ham. Serve immediately.

Serves 4 to 6

Honey-Mustard Chicken

4   skinned and boned
     chicken breasts

3   tablespoons Dijon
     mustard

¼   cup honey

½   teaspoon curry powder

2   tablespoons butter or
     margarine, melted

- Arrange chicken in a shallow
  baking dish.

- Combine mustard and next
  3 ingredients and pour over
  chicken.

- Bake at 350° for 45 to 60 minutes.
  Serve immediately.

Serves 4

Local honeys help build resistance to pollens and other allergens when eaten regularly.

What Can I Bring?

Ashburn Chicken

8   chicken breasts

½   garlic bulb, pureed

2   tablespoons dried
     oregano

    Salt and pepper to taste

¼   cup red wine vinegar

¼   cup olive oil

½   cup pitted prunes

¼   cup pitted Spanish green
     olives (without
     pimientos)

¼   cup capers, undrained

3   bay leaves

½   cup firmly packed
     brown sugar

½   cup white wine

    Garnish: 2 tablespoons
     chopped fresh parsley
     or cilantro

- Combine first 10 ingredients in a shallow dish; cover and chill overnight.

- Arrange chicken in a single layer in a 9 x 13 x 2-inch baking dish and pour marinade over top. Sprinkle with brown sugar and pour wine over top.

- Bake at 350° for 50 to 60 minutes.

- Transfer chicken to a serving platter. Garnish, if desired. Serve hot or at room temperature.

Serves 8

Arlington Almond Chicken

½ cup grated Parmesan cheese

½ teaspoon garlic powder

½ teaspoon poultry seasoning

½ teaspoon paprika

½ teaspoon dried dill weed

¼ teaspoon pepper

4-6 skinned and boned chicken breasts

1 cup sliced almonds

- Combine first 6 ingredients in a zip-top plastic bag. Place 1 chicken breast in bag; seal and shake to coat. Place chicken on a greased baking sheet. Press almonds onto top of chicken.

- Repeat procedure with remaining chicken breasts.

- Bake at 350° for 20 minutes.

Serves 4

*O*nly 25½ square miles in size, Arlington is the third smallest county in the nation but looms enormously in the historical sense. Carved out of Alexandria in the early 1930s, the county took its name from Robert E. Lee's home, today the central structure of the Arlington National Cemetery. The mansion was built by George Washington Parke Custis whose daughter married Robert E. Lee. In 1955, Congress officially designated the mansion as Lee's permanent national memorial honoring his greatness.

Crisp and Tangy Chicken

1	large egg
¼	teaspoon pepper
1½	teaspoons poultry seasoning
4	teaspoons salt
½	cup vegetable oil
1	cup apple cider vinegar
4	bone-in split chicken breasts or equal amounts chicken pieces

- Combine first 6 ingredients, reserving ¾ cup.

- Combine chicken and remaining marinade in a large heavy-duty zip-top plastic bag. Seal and chill 12 hours.

- Grill chicken over medium-low heat (325° to 350°) 1½ to 2 hours, turning and basting with reserved ¾ cup marinade every 15 minutes. Chicken skin should be dark and crispy and the inside should be tender and juicy.

Serves 4

To gauge the readiness of coals for grilling, hold your hand, palm side down, a few inches above the coals. Count the number of seconds you are able to comfortably leave your hand there:

2 seconds = hot (400° to 450° F)

3 seconds = medium-hot (375° to 400° F)

4 seconds = medium (350° to 375° F)

5 seconds = medium-low (325° to 350° F)

6 seconds = low (300° to 325° F)

Marinated Pork Tenderloin with Mustard Sauce

¾   cup soy sauce

¾   cup Marsala wine

2¼ tablespoons minced garlic

2¼ teaspoons ground ginger

1½ tablespoons dry mustard

1½ teaspoons ground thyme

1   pork tenderloin or loin roast

    Mustard Sauce (see below)

- Whisk first 6 ingredients. Reserve ⅓ of marinade to use for basting.

- Combine marinade and pork in a large heavy-duty zip-top plastic bag. Seal and chill overnight.

- Remove pork from marinade, discarding marinade.

- Grill pork over medium heat (350° to 375°) for 30 minutes, or bake at 350° for 30 minutes or until meat thermometer registers 170°.

Serves 4

Mustard Sauce

1   teaspoon dry mustard

1   tablespoon honey mustard

½   cup sour cream

½   cup mayonnaise

2   green onions, finely chopped

1½ tablespoons red wine vinegar

    Salt and pepper to taste

- Combine all ingredients.

Ginger Pork Steaks

2	beef bouillon cubes
½	cup hot water
¼	cup honey
¼	cup soy sauce
1	teaspoon sugar
1	teaspoon salt
1	teaspoon freshly grated ginger
6	pork steaks or loin chops

- Combine bouillon cubes and ½ cup hot water, stirring until dissolved. Add honey and next 4 ingredients, stirring well.

- Place steaks in a shallow baking dish; pour marinade over top. Cover and chill 6 hours, turning occasionally. Remove steaks from marinade, discarding marinade.

- Grill steaks over medium heat (350° to 375°) 15 minutes or until done.

Serves 4 to 6

Marinated Pork Tenderloin with Dried Fruit

1	boneless pork loin or tenderloin (about 2⅓ pounds; if using loin cut in half lengthwise)
3	tablespoons olive oil
	Coarse-grain sea salt
1½	cups Port
1	cup fresh orange juice
3	tablespoons honey or maple syrup
3	tablespoons cider vinegar
2	tablespoons fresh or 2 teaspoons dried rosemary
3	shallots or 1 small onion, minced
3	garlic cloves, halved
½	cup dried apricots, halved
½	cup pitted prunes, halved
	Salt and pepper to taste

- Rub pork on all sides with oil and coarse-grain salt; place in a 5- to 6-inch deep bowl or pan.

- Simmer Port and next 9 ingredients in a saucepan 5 minutes; pour over pork. Cool to room temperature. Cover and chill at least 4 hours.

- Remove pork from marinade 1 to 1½ hours before serving, reserving marinade. Chill pork.

- Bring marinade to a boil. Reduce heat and simmer 30 minutes or until reduced to consistency of thin gravy.

- Grill pork over medium heat (350° to 375°) 30 minutes, or bake at 350° for 30 minutes. Do not overcook.

- Slice and serve with marinade.

Serves 4 to 5

Spareribs

1   teaspoon dry mustard

¼   teaspoon pepper

Liberal sprinkle of garlic powder

½   cup sugar

1   teaspoon salt

2   teaspoons Worcestershire sauce

½   cup ketchup

½   cup vinegar

2   pounds baby back ribs (approximately 3 racks)

- Combine first 5 ingredients; add Worcestershire sauce, ketchup, and vinegar, stirring well.
- Broil ribs until browned on both sides; drain fat.
- Place ribs in a roasting pan and pour sauce over top.
- Bake at 350° for 2 hours, basting often.

Serves 6

Microwave damp scented hand towels if your guests are enjoying messy finger foods. Arrange rolled towels on a platter, and at the end of the meal, serve your guests. Your gesture will be appreciated, and your warmth will be conveyed as they wrap the towel around their hands.

Easy Apple-Glazed Pork Chops

4 (1-inch-thick) boneless pork chops

Salt and pepper to taste

1 teaspoon dried rosemary

3 teaspoons olive oil

⅓ cup white wine

2 garlic cloves, minced

⅓ cup apple juice concentrate

1 teaspoon apple cider vinegar

2 fresh rosemary sprigs, divided

- Season pork chops on both sides with salt, pepper, and dried rosemary.

- Brown pork chops in hot oil in a nonstick skillet over medium-high heat 2 minutes on each side. Reduce heat to low and cook 4 minutes. Remove pork chops to a platter.

- Add wine and garlic to skillet; bring to a boil over high heat. Boil until liquid is reduced by half. Add juice concentrate, vinegar, leaves of 1 fresh rosemary sprig, and pork chop juice from platter. Boil, stirring constantly, until mixture is bubbly and thickened.

- Pour glaze over chops. Garnish with remaining fresh rosemary sprig.

- Serve with Sour Cream Mashed Potatoes, Glazed Carrots, or Baby peas.

Serves 4

The quickest way to chill anything (about 10 minutes) is to immerse it in a mixture of half ice and half water. Caution: Do not put carbonated beverages or champagne in the freezer. If forgotten, they can explode.

Roast Pork Calypso

1 (5- to 6-pound) pork
roast, trimmed

1 large onion, chopped

2 garlic cloves, crushed

1 teaspoon salt

1 teaspoon ground ginger

½ teaspoon ground pepper

2 bay leaves

1 cup dark rum

Beef broth

- Brown pork in a large ovenproof Dutch oven; drain fat.

- Add onion and garlic. Cook until browned. Add salt, next 4 ingredients, and beef broth to cover.

- Bake, covered, at 300° for 3 to 4 hours.

*Serves 8 as a main dish
and 16 as an appetizer*

This Earth Day, plant a fruit tree. Some suggestions are apple, lemon, peach, pear, and plum. In the spring, you will have blossoms. In the summer, you can enjoy the shade. Fall will give you fruit. And winter will delight your sense of smell when pruned branches are put in the fireplace.

Tangy Fruit Pork Chops

1	tablespoon butter or margarine
4	boneless pork chops
½	cup raspberry preserves or jam (or favorite flavor)
3	tablespoons Dijon mustard
1	tablespoon raspberry or white vinegar

- Melt butter in a skillet over medium heat; add pork chops and brown on both sides.

- Combine preserves, mustard, and vinegar. Pour over pork chops. Cover, reduce heat, and simmer 5 minutes.

- Serve with rice, cornbread, green beans, or carrots for an easy weekday dinner.

Serves 4

*S*end creative invitations to set the mood or atmosphere for the party. Your guests will be delighted at the effort and eagerly await what is in store for them.

Pork Tenderloin Stuffed with Dried Fruit

1   cup pitted prunes

1   cup dried apricots

½   cup butter or margarine, softened

4   pounds boned pork tenderloin, prepared for stuffing

1   garlic clove, slivered

Salt and pepper to taste

1   tablespoon dried thyme

1   cup Madeira wine

1   tablespoon molasses

- Preheat oven to 350°.

- Make a paste of first 3 ingredients and spread on pork. Make small slits in pork and place garlic slivers in slits. Roll pork up, jelly roll fashion, and tie with string. Place in a roasting pan. Season with salt and pepper; sprinkle with thyme.

- Combine wine and molasses and pour over pork.

- Bake at 350° for 1 hour and 20 minutes (20 minutes per pound), basting occasionally with juices.

- Remove from oven. Let stand at room temperature covered with aluminum foil 15 to 20 minutes before serving.

- Slice thinly and serve on a platter.

Serves 8 to 10

Ask butcher to prepare pork tenderloin for stuffing.

Put extra prunes into the brown sugar container to keep it moist.

Grilled Pepper Tuna with Cilantro Butter

4   (¾-inch-thick) fresh tuna
     steaks

¼   cup extra-virgin olive oil

1½ tablespoons freshly
     cracked pepper

½   cup unsalted butter,
     softened

2   tablespoons chopped
     fresh cilantro

1   tablespoon chopped
     fresh parsley

¼   teaspoon salt

¼   teaspoon freshly ground
     pepper

1   teaspoon grated lime or
     lemon rind

1½ tablespoons fresh lime
     or lemon juice

- Brush tuna steaks lightly with
  oil and press liberally with
  1½ tablespoons cracked pepper.

- Grill on a greased rack 8 to
  10 minutes on each side or until
  fish is white.

- Process butter and remaining
  ingredients in a food processor
  until blended. Transfer mixture to
  a sheet of plastic wrap and form
  into a log. Chill until firm.

- Slice prepared butter and serve
  over hot fish.

Serves 4

Crab Cakes with Creole Sauce

1	large egg
3	teaspoons whipping cream
1	teaspoon dry sherry
½	teaspoon salt
1	teaspoon dried parsley
¼	teaspoon ground red pepper
1	pound fresh lump crabmeat, drained
1½	teaspoons all-purpose flour
2	dashes of hot pepper sauce, or to taste
4	tablespoons butter or margarine
2	tablespoons olive oil
	Creole Sauce

- Combine first 9 ingredients and fashion into 4 large or 6 to 8 small cakes.

- Melt butter and heat oil in a skillet over medium-high heat; add cakes and sauté until golden brown.

- Serve crab cakes with Creole Sauce.

Serves 4

(Crab Cakes with Creole Sauce continued)

Creole Sauce

¼	cup fresh lemon juice
¼	cup prepared horseradish
2	teaspoons chopped green onions
2	teaspoons chopped celery
2	teaspoons chopped green bell pepper
2	garlic cloves
1	teaspoon chopped fresh parsley
½	teaspoon salt
½	cup olive oil
	Hot sauce to taste
	Red pepper flakes to taste

• Process all ingredients in a food processor until blended.

Several days before the gathering and after the menu is planned, write the recipes on pretty cards and have them ready for your guests when they ask. It will save you time and be convenient for them.

Seafood Lasagna

6	cups water
2	pounds unpeeled, medium-size fresh shrimp
12	uncooked lasagna noodles
2	tablespoons butter or margarine
1	cup chopped onion
1	(8-ounce) package cream cheese, softened
1½	cups small curd cottage cheese
1	large egg, lightly beaten
2	teaspoons dried basil, crushed
½	teaspoon salt
⅛	teaspoon pepper
¼	cup butter or margarine
¼	cup all-purpose flour
2	cups milk
⅔	cup Chablis or dry white wine
1	(6-ounce) can crabmeat, drained
¼	cup grated Parmesan cheese
½	cup (2 ounces) shredded cheddar cheese
	Garnish: chopped fresh parsley

- Bring 6 cups water to a boil in a Dutch oven; add shrimp and cook 3 to 5 minutes. Drain well; rinse with cold water and drain. Chill. Peel shrimp and devein, if desired. Coarsely chop shrimp; set aside.

- Cook lasagna noodles according to package directions; drain well. Rinse with cold water and set aside.

- Melt 2 tablespoons butter in a skillet over medium heat; add onion and sauté until tender. Add cream cheese. Reduce heat to low and cook, stirring occasionally, until cream cheese melts. Stir in cottage cheese and next 4 ingredients. Remove from heat and set aside.

- Melt ¼ cup butter in a heavy saucepan over low heat; add flour, stirring until smooth. Gradually add milk; cook over medium heat, stirring constantly, until mixture is thickened and bubbly. Remove from heat; stir in reserved shrimp, wine, and crabmeat.

- Drain noodles and layer half in a greased 9 x 13 x 2-inch baking dish. Spread half of cream cheese mixture over noodles; top with half of shrimp mixture. Repeat

(Seafood Lasagna continued)

layers with remaining noodles, cream cheese mixture, and shrimp mixture. Sprinkle with Parmesan cheese.

- Bake at 350° for 45 minutes.

- Sprinkle with cheddar cheese. Bake 5 more minutes or until cheese is melted. Let stand at room temperature 10 minutes before serving. Garnish, if desired.

Serves 8

Simply Sensational Scallops

2	tablespoons margarine
1	pound bay scallops, rinsed and patted dry
⅜	cup breadcrumbs
2	teaspoons dried oregano
½	teaspoon salt
½	teaspoon ground black pepper
½	teaspoon garlic powder
½	teaspoon Cajun seasoning
½	teaspoon paprika
1	lemon, cut into wedges

- Broil margarine in a broiling pan until bubbly but not brown.

- Add scallops to margarine, tossing to coat.

- Sprinkle scallops with breadcrumbs and next 5 ingredients, tossing to coat. Sprinkle with paprika.

- Broil on the second oven rack 8 to 9 minutes. Serve with lemon wedges.

Serves 2

Salmon Wellington

1½ pounds fresh salmon
     fillets, skinned and
     boned

½ teaspoon dried dill weed

1¼ pounds frozen chopped
     spinach (2 packages)

4 ounces feta cheese,
     crumbled

8 phyllo dough sheets
     Butter-flavored cooking
     spray

- Cut salmon into 4 (6-ounce) pieces and sprinkle evenly with dill weed.

- Microwave spinach according to package directions; drain well and divide into 4 equal portions. Spread 1 spinach portion over each piece of salmon; top evenly with feta.

- Thaw phyllo sheets according to package directions; spray half of each sheet with cooking spray, 1 at a time. Fold each in half and spray the top with cooking spray. Place 2 folded sheets together and place a salmon stack, feta side down, on the center of each section of phyllo. Fold phyllo over salmon, covering completely; fold ends over to seal and place seam side down on a nonstick baking sheet.

- Bake at 350° for 25 to 30 minutes or until golden brown.

Serves 4

Adults delight in receiving a small gift to take home after a party. Homemade goodies, a small trinket that fits your theme, or one of the small potted plants you grouped together as a centerpiece are the sort of thoughtful tokens your guests will have the next day as a reminder of the time that was shared with you.

Salmon with Yogurt-Dill Sauce

2	cups water
2	cups wine vinegar
1	small to medium onion, sliced
¼	teaspoon freshly ground pepper
4	salmon fillets (1½ to 2 pounds)
	Yogurt-Dill Sauce

- Bring first 4 ingredients to a boil in a 2-quart saucepan. Add salmon and simmer 10 minutes per inch of thickness at thickest part or until done, turning once if liquid does not cover fish.
- Remove fish from liquid and chill, if desired. Serve with Yogurt-Dill Sauce.

Serves 4

Yogurt-Dill Sauce

⅓	cup nonfat plain yogurt
⅓	cup nonfat mayonnaise
2	tablespoons chopped fresh parsley
1	tablespoon chopped green onions
1	teaspoon lemon juice
¼	teaspoon dried dill weed

- Combine all ingredients and chill.

To add a touch of class to your iced tea, run a lemon wedge around the rim, and then dip in sugar. Garnish with a sprig of fresh mint.

Lime Broiled Salmon Steaks

⅜ cup lime juice

3 tablespoons vegetable oil

1½ teaspoons Dijon mustard

1 tablespoon grated fresh ginger

⅜ teaspoon ground red pepper

Freshly ground black pepper to taste

4 (8-ounce) salmon steaks

- Combine first 6 ingredients in a shallow dish; add salmon and marinate 30 to 60 minutes, turning occasionally.

- Remove salmon from marinade, discarding marinade. Grill over charcoal 5 minutes on each side or until firm, basting often with marinade.

Serves 4

Leftover salmon steaks can be flaked and tossed with your favorite pasta or salad, or pureed and spread on crackers.

Grilled Garlic Shrimp

1	pound unpeeled, large fresh shrimp
2	tablespoons soy sauce
1	tablespoon peanut oil
1	tablespoon vegetable oil
3	garlic cloves, minced
¼	teaspoon crushed red pepper flakes
3	green onions, cut into 1-inch pieces

- Soak 4 (12-inch) bamboo skewers in water to cover 20 minutes.
- Peel shrimp and devein, if desired; place in a large zip-top plastic bag.
- Combine soy sauce and next 4 ingredients; pour over shrimp. Seal and chill 15 minutes.
- Drain shrimp, discarding marinade. Thread shrimp and green onions alternately on skewers.
- Grill or broil 2½ minutes on each side or until shrimp are opaque.

Serves 4

Spraying your barbecue grill with nonstick cooking spray prevents food from sticking and makes cleanup easier. Remember: hot grill, cold spray, food won't stick.

Crab Imperial

2 tablespoons butter or margarine

2 tablespoons all-purpose flour

1 cup milk or half-and-half

¼ teaspoon dry mustard

1 teaspoon salt

¼ teaspoon black pepper

¼ teaspoon celery salt

Pinch of dried thyme

Dash of garlic salt

1 tablespoon minced onion

2 tablespoons capers

Several dashes of hot sauce

Several dashes of Worcestershire sauce

Dash of ground red pepper

1 tablespoon chopped fresh parsley

1 tablespoon sherry

1 pound backfin crabmeat, drained

2 egg yolks, lightly beaten

Breadcrumbs

• Cook first 14 ingredients in a medium saucepan over medium-low heat, stirring occasionally, until thickened. Stir in parsley and next 3 ingredients.

• Transfer mixture to a lightly greased 1½- to 2-quart baking dish. Sprinkle with breadcrumbs.

• Bake at 400° for 10 to 15 minutes or until golden brown.

Serves 6

*A*lways separate eggs while they are cold-just out of the refrigerator. Cold eggs are easier to separate.

Northern Neck Crab Cakes

1   pound backfin crabmeat, drained

1   large egg, lightly beaten

½   cup breadcrumbs

2   tablespoons mayonnaise

1   teaspoon Dijon mustard

1   teaspoon Worcestershire sauce

1   teaspoon seafood seasoning

1   teaspoon cider vinegar

2   tablespoons butter or margarine, melted

2   tablespoons milk

1   tablespoon chopped fresh parsley

- Thoroughly combine all ingredients in a large bowl. Form into 6 cakes.

- Sauté cakes in a nonstick skillet over medium-low heat 5 minutes on each side.

Serves 3 to 4

Nonfat yogurt may be substituted for mayonnaise for a low-fat version.

When taking fresh flowers from a garden to a gathering, store the flowers in a raw potato to keep them fresh. Slice the potato in half lengthwise, and place the halves around the stems; hold together with a rubber band. Voila! Flowers for the hostess and the potato for the compost.

Fairfax Station Shrimp Over Fettuccine

3   teaspoons butter or margarine, divided

2   carrots, sliced

4   ounces pea pods or snap peas

1   garlic clove, minced

1   (8-ounce) package frozen shrimp or 8 ounces peeled and deveined fresh shrimp

1   tablespoon all-purpose flour

½   teaspoon salt

½   teaspoon pepper

1   cup skim milk

8   ounces spinach fettuccine, cooked

¼   cup chopped fresh parsley

1   tablespoon grated Parmesan cheese

- Melt 2 teaspoons butter in a skillet over medium heat; add carrot, pea pods, and garlic, and sauté 5 minutes. Remove vegetables from skillet, reserving drippings; set vegetables aside.

- Add remaining 1 teaspoon butter and shrimp to drippings. Sauté 3 minutes. Sprinkle flour over mixture, stirring well. Add salt and pepper. Add milk and cook until thickened and bubbly, stirring occasionally. Add reserved vegetables, stirring well.

- Serve over hot cooked fettuccine. Sprinkle with parsley and Parmesan cheese.

Serves 4

*T*he American Red Cross was founded in Fairfax Station. In the fields surrounding St. Mary's Catholic Church, Clara Barton administered help to the wounded of the Civil War. The little white clapboard church and some of the land around the church has been preserved so we can imagine the scenes of chaos in the wilderness that she must have faced.

Cajun Chicken and Shrimp Over Pasta

1	tablespoon garlic, minced
4	tablespoons butter or margarine
4-6	boneless, skinless chicken breasts, cubed
1	pound medium shrimp, cleaned and deveined
1	tablespoon Cajun spice seasoning (see note)
1	red bell pepper, cored, seeded, and diced
½	cup scallions, sliced
1	cup heavy cream
1-2	tablespoons cornstarch
1	(16-ounce) package spaghetti
2	tablespoons fresh parsley
	Freshly grated Parmesan cheese
1	tablespoon of Kitchen Bouquet or Worcestershire sauce

- Cook garlic in butter for 30 seconds using a large skillet.

- Add chicken and Cajun spices and cook until browned. Add shrimp and cook until pink (3 to 5 minutes). Sprinkle additional Cajun spices on top (use sparingly). Add red pepper and scallions and cook 2 to 3 minutes. Add cornstarch to heavy cream in a bowl and beat until thickened (using a wire whisk). Add cream to skillet (and additional Cajun spices if you like it hot), and turn heat to medium-high and cook until thickened. Add Kitchen Bouquet or Worcestershire sauce and stir together.

- While sauce is cooking, cook spaghetti according to package directions and drain.

- Place spaghetti in a serving dish and top with chicken and shrimp mixture.

- Serve with fresh parsley and freshly grated Parmesan cheese.

Serves 4 to 6

You can find Cajun spice seasoning in your local market. There are many kinds, all with their own distinct characteristics. They usually include garlic, onion, chiles, black pepper, mustard and celery.

Feta Shrimp

1½ pounds unpeeled,
      medium-size fresh
      shrimp
3   garlic cloves, chopped
1   tablespoon olive oil
2   tablespoons white wine
1   (16-ounce) can diced
      tomatoes, drained
      Dash of salt
      Dash of ground white
      pepper
2   tablespoons chopped
      fresh parsley
¼   cup crumbled feta
      cheese
      Hot cooked rice

- Peel shrimp. Devein, if desired.
- Sauté shrimp and garlic in hot oil in a skillet; add wine and cook until shrimp is opaque.
- Transfer to a serving dish. Top mixture with tomatoes; add salt, pepper, and parsley. Sprinkle with feta.
- Serve over hot cooked rice.

Serves 3 to 4

Pecan-Crusted Fish

1	cup pecan pieces
¼	teaspoon pepper
1	tablespoon lemon thyme, parsley, or oregano
	Salt to taste
2	large eggs or ½ cup egg substitute
¼	cup milk
1	teaspoon ground red pepper
1-2	pounds catfish or other white fish fillets
3	tablespoons butter or margarine
1	lemon
	Garnish: lemon slices

- Process first 4 ingredients in a food processor until finely chopped; transfer mixture to a shallow dish.
- Combine eggs, milk, and red pepper in a bowl.
- Dip fillets in egg mixture and dredge in pecan mixture, coating thickly on both sides.
- Melt butter in a nonstick skillet over medium heat; add fillets and cook until done, turning once and being careful not to burn pecans. Squeeze lemon juice over fillets while cooking. Garnish, if desired.

Serves 4

Gardening fishermen can try this technique taught to the early settlers by Native American Indians: Freeze fish bones and waste until planting season; then sow some of the fish underneath vegetables such as tomatoes. Watch them grow.

Rosemary Lamb Chops

½ cup olive oil

½ cup best-quality soy sauce

½ cup balsamic vinegar

8 garlic cloves, minced

4 teaspoons dried rosemary, crushed

8 (¾-inch-thick) lamb chops

- Whisk together first 5 ingredients.
- Place lamb chops in a 9 x 13 x 2-inch pan. Pour marinade over top. Let stand at room temperature 30 to 45 minutes or chill 2 to 3 hours. Remove chops from marinade, discarding marinade.
- Grill over medium heat (350° to 375°) 3 to 4 minutes on each side for medium rare.

Serves 4

Veal Scaloppine

½ cup all-purpose flour
Salt and pepper to taste
2½ pounds veal scaloppine
3 tablespoons butter or
   margarine, divided
1 pound fresh
   mushrooms, sliced
1 medium-size green bell
   pepper, seeded and
   chopped
2 cans chicken broth
1 (8-ounce) can tomato
   sauce
½ cup white wine

- Combine flour, salt, and pepper to taste in a shallow dish; dredge veal in mixture.
- Melt 2 tablespoons butter in a skillet over medium heat; add veal. Cook until lightly browned. Transfer veal to a baking dish.
- Melt remaining 1 tablespoon butter in skillet; add mushrooms and bell pepper. Sauté until tender. Stir in broth and tomato sauce. Stir in wine and bring to a boil. Reduce heat and simmer 5 minutes. Pour sauce over veal.
- Bake at 350° for 45 minutes.

Serves 6 to 8

Tradition says to do a Maypole dance, join hands and dance around the decorated Maypole while singing your favorite songs. Then each girl searches for seven different flowers to place under her pillow that night. If this is done, she will dream of her future husband.

Marinade for Beef or Chicken

1½   cups vegetable oil

¾   cup soy sauce

¼   cup Worcestershire
      sauce

2   teaspoons dry mustard

2¼   teaspoons salt

1   teaspoon pepper

1½   cups red wine vinegar

1½   teaspoons dried parsley
      flakes

⅓   cup lemon juice

2   garlic cloves, crushed

- Whisk together all ingredients.
  Pour over beef or chicken and
  chill several hours or overnight.
- Grill meat as desired.

Yields 4 cups

Recent concerns about food safety have made us all aware of the need to avoid cross-contamination with raw and cooked meats, poultry, and seafood. In compiling What Can I Bring?*, we've adjusted recipes to guarantee ample marinade. We've increased marinade ingredients by ⅓, and called for discarding used marinade. During cooking, we provide reserved "fresh" marinade for basting. We encourage you to make these same adjustments in your "tried and true" favorites, for safety's sake.*

All-Purpose Marinade
(for Chicken, Shrimp, or Tofu)

1	cup orange or grapefruit juice
3	tablespoons sesame oil
3	tablespoons olive oil
¼	cup tamari or soy sauce
4	garlic cloves, crushed
1	teaspoon dried rosemary or oregano
¼	teaspoon freshly ground black pepper
	Juice of 1 lime (optional)

• Combine first 7 ingredients including lime juice, if using. For chicken, marinate in the refrigerator overnight. For shrimp or other seafood, marinate 30 minutes. For tofu, marinate 15 minutes. Grill, broil, or sauté as desired.

Meats marinate best in cold temperatures. Keep marinating meats in the refrigerator until time to cook them. Also, remember to cook meats for an additional 3 to 5 minutes after the final marinade is applied.

Sauce for Ham

¼ cup sour cream

¼ cup mayonnaise

2 tablespoons Dijon mustard

2 tablespoons prepared horseradish

Dash of salt

1 teaspoon lemon juice

1 tablespoon chopped fresh chives

• Combine all ingredients. Chill at least 1 hour.

• Serve with ham. It's also great to use with leftovers on sandwiches.

Serves 6

*H*osting an adult Easter Egg Hunt is filled with rewards. Plastic eggs are filled with anything from lottery tickets to movie coupons to small liquor bottles to slips of paper with descriptions of white elephant gifts to traditional candy. At the last minute, hide the hard-cooked colored eggs (remember to count them) and the plastic eggs. When all the eggs have been discovered, have the guests come inside and create a deviled egg assembly line. The guests get to know one another as each task is performed. Those who have not had an occasion to hunt eggs enjoy, and those who have not hunted in years will enjoy a new version. Ask each guest to bring a basket or bag and some eggs.

Soups and Stews

Wintry, Warm
and Wonderful Supper

Sun-Dried Tomato Spread, *page 19*

Hearty Chili, *page 110*

Southern Corn Pudding, *page 196*

Green Salad with
Curry-Almond Dressing, *page 232*

Chocolate Fudge Brownies, *page 239*

Let It Snow,
Let It Snow, Let It Snow

In some regions, major snows are a matter-of-fact part of winter life, but here in Northern Virginia where we are blanketed with the white stuff only occasionally, it is a cause for celebration. Armed with the joy of an unexpected holiday due to closed schools and offices and unplowed roads, we spill out of our homes and take to the streets and parks. Strolling our neighborhoods, we lend a hand with snow shoveling here or dig out a car there. Roused from our winter hibernations, we catch up on neighborhood news. On sleds, cross-country skis, and other contraptions born of invention, we attack the snow, trying to get our fill of it while it lasts.

All this winter fun translates to rosy cheeks, frosty toes and fingers, and hearty appetites! Pull out the soup pot and concoct a hearty soup or stew that will simmer on the back of the stove for hours while you play. Organize an impromptu neighborhood potluck. *"What Can I Bring?"* your neighbors ask. You never know what treasures are stashed away in pantries and freezers. As darkness falls, we gather round for a hearty, casual supper. The little ones wind down with games and stories, the grown-ups relax with libations, and all enjoy a robust meal heightened by a day of exercise. At the end of the evening, we bundle up to trudge home. Kids half-heartedly throw one last snowball, couples walk arm in arm through the moonlit hush of the snow, and all are content. Tomorrow the world will slowly return to normal, but for one day, we truly had a winter paradise here in Northern Virginia.

What Can I Bring?

*S*et up a snow emergency closet. Save some projects for your children for the time when the novelty of a snowstorm wears off. Include the following ingredients, being sure to shop ahead of time!

- Cardboard
- String
- Glitter
- Stapler
- Stickers
- Glue and tape
- Scraps of sewing notions (ribbon, fabric, lace, rickrack)
- Scissors
- Old greeting cards for cutouts
- Pipe cleaners
- Crayons, colored pencils, markers
- Construction paper
- Wooden craft sticks
- Egg cartons
- Clean Styrofoam meat trays

French Onion Soup

12 French bread slices

- Let bread slices stand at room temperature covered loosely with a dish towel 5 hours on each side. Or place in a single layer on a baking sheet and bake at 300° for 5 to 8 minutes on each side or until dry.

½ cup butter or margarine
3 pounds onions, halved
7 cups beef broth
1¼ cups water
9 ounces finely shredded Gruyère cheese
½ cup dry sherry
  Freshly ground pepper to taste

- Melt butter in a large Dutch oven over medium heat.
- Cut heels off of onion halves and slice crosswise. Add onion slices to butter. Cook over low heat, stirring often, 45 to 60 minutes. Add broth and 1¼ cups water to onion; bring to a boil. Reduce heat and simmer 15 minutes.
- Preheat oven to 400°.
- Place bread slices on a baking sheet; top evenly with cheese.
- Bake at 400° for 4 minutes or until cheese is melted and lightly brown.
- Add sherry and pepper to soup. Bring to a boil.
- Ladle soup into individual serving bowls and top each bowl with 2 bread slices. Serve immediately.

Serves 6

Tips to remove onion or garlic odor from your hands.

- *Put your fingers on something made of stainless steel (sink faucet, spoon) and run cold water over them.*
- *Rub lemon juice on your hands.*

Cream of Carrot and Lemon Soup

6   tablespoons unsalted
      butter, divided
1   large onion, chopped
1   garlic clove, minced
1½   pounds carrots, peeled
      and sliced
3   tomatoes, peeled and
      chopped
1   baking potato, peeled
      and sliced
¼   cup shredded fresh basil
4   cups chicken stock or
      3 cups canned chicken
      broth diluted with
      1 cup water
1½   teaspoons salt
¼   teaspoon freshly ground
      pepper
1   cup crème fraîche
¼   teaspoon hot sauce
¼   cup lemon juice
      Garnishes: carrot curls,
      crème fraîche, fresh
      parsley sprigs

- Melt 4 tablespoons butter in a large saucepan over medium heat; add onion and garlic. Cover and cook over low heat 5 minutes or until tender. Add remaining 2 tablespoons butter, carrots, and next 6 ingredients. Bring to a boil; cover, reduce heat, and simmer 45 minutes.

- Puree carrot mixture in a blender until smooth.

- Add crème fraîche and hot sauce to puree; return to saucepan and simmer 15 minutes. Cover and chill overnight, if desired.

- Reheat soup and stir in lemon juice when ready to serve. Garnish, if desired.

Serves 6 to 8

You can purchase crème fraîche at a gourmet market or make your own. Whisk together 1 cup heavy cream and 1 cup sour cream in a bowl. Cover loosely and let stand in a warm place overnight. Cover and chill at least 4 hours. The crème fraîche will be quite thick.

White Chili

1	medium onion, chopped
1	garlic clove, minced
1	teaspoon ground cumin
1	tablespoon canola oil
1	(15- to 19-ounce) can cannellini beans, drained
1	(15- to 19-ounce) can garbanzo beans, drained
1	(4-ounce) can green chiles, chopped
2	skinned and boned chicken breasts, cut into 1-inch cubes
1	(12-ounce) can white corn, drained
1½	cups chicken broth
1	cup (4 ounces) shredded Monterey Jack cheese
	Toppings: sour cream, hot sauce

- Preheat oven to 350°.
- Cook first 3 ingredients in hot oil in a saucepan over medium heat until tender.
- Combine onion mixture, cannellini beans, and next 5 ingredients in a 2½-quart baking dish.
- Bake, covered, at 350° for 1 hour or until chicken is tender.
- Top each serving with shredded cheese and desired toppings.

Serves 8

If you're snowbound and celebrating with a cabin-fever party, set up a white theme and serve this chili.
To carry on this winter wonderland focus, use your saved plastic mustard and jelly squeeze bottles, fill with colored water, and send the children-(big and little)-outside to paint the snow!

Winter Vegetable Soup

5	medium carrots, peeled and sliced
5	medium potatoes, peeled and cubed
5	medium onions, chopped
2	leeks, trimmed and chopped
¾	cup butter or margarine
½	tablespoon salt
½	tablespoon ground white pepper
5	tomatoes, chopped
1	(8-ounce) package fresh mushrooms, sliced
1	cup half-and-half
2	tablespoons chopped fresh parsley

- Combine first 7 ingredients. Cover with water and bring to a boil in a large Dutch oven. Reduce heat and simmer 25 minutes or until vegetables are tender. Remove from heat.

- Puree two-thirds of vegetable mixture in a food processor until smooth and return to Dutch oven stirring well.

- Add tomatoes and mushrooms to soup; simmer 15 minutes. Stir in half-and-half and parsley; cook until thoroughly heated. Serve hot.

Serves 6 to 8

*O*nions should be stored in a cool, dark place where air can circulate around them.

Potatoes should never be stored in a refrigerator. They will have a sweet taste if kept in cold temperatures.

Carrots should never be stored near apples. The carrots will get a bitter taste.

Shrimp Jambalaya

2	pounds unpeeled, medium-size fresh shrimp
2	tablespoons vegetable oil
1	cup chopped onion
½	cup chopped green bell pepper
1	carrot, cut into thin strips
¾	cup chopped celery
4	garlic cloves, minced
1	(8-ounce) can tomato sauce
1	(14½-ounce) can tomatoes, undrained and chopped
1	(14½-ounce) can ready-to-serve chicken broth
1½	cups water
1	cup uncooked long-grain rice
1	teaspoon salt
½	teaspoon dried thyme
½	teaspoon ground red pepper
¼	teaspoon chili powder
¼	teaspoon sugar
½	cup chopped fresh parsley
⅛	teaspoon hot sauce (optional)

- Peel shrimp. Devein, if desired. Cook shrimp in hot oil in a Dutch oven over medium heat, stirring constantly, 5 minutes or until shrimp turn pink. Remove shrimp with a slotted spoon, reserving drippings; chill shrimp.

- Add onion and next 4 ingredients to drippings; cook over medium heat 3 minutes. Stir in tomato sauce and next 9 ingredients; bring to a boil. Cover, reduce heat and simmer, stirring often, 45 minutes or until rice is tender and most of liquid is absorbed.

- Stir in parsley, shrimp, and, if desired, hot sauce. Cook 10 minutes or until thoroughly heated.

Serves 8 to 10

Easy Broccoli Soup

½	cup butter or margarine
2	tablespoons grated onion
¼	cup all-purpose flour
1	cup milk
1	cup half-and-half
2	cups chicken broth
½	teaspoon salt
¼	teaspoon garlic powder
½	teaspoon dried whole basil
1	head fresh broccoli, chopped (3 cups)
	Garnish: shredded cheddar cheese

• Melt butter in a saucepan over medium heat; add onion and sauté until tender. Add flour and cook, stirring constantly, until roux is beige-colored. Add milk and next 6 ingredients; cook over medium heat, stirring often, until soup is thickened.

• Chill overnight, if desired. Reheat to serve and garnish, if desired.

Serves 6 to 8

Purchase green, tight heads of broccoli buds. Any other color means that the vegetable is past its prime.

Tavern Tortilla Soup

1 tablespoon butter or margarine

1 medium-size purple onion, chopped

1 garlic clove, minced

2 (14½-ounce) cans chicken or vegetable broth

1 (8-ounce) can tomato sauce

1 (28-ounce) can diced tomatoes

1 (4.5-ounce) can chopped green chiles, drained

1 (15-ounce) can black beans, drained

1 (4-ounce) can yellow corn kernels, drained

¼ cup cilantro, chopped

¼ teaspoon crushed sweet red pepper flakes

1 teaspoon dried oregano

6 corn tortillas, cut into ½-inch-wide strips

Vegetable oil

1 cup (4 ounces) shredded Monterey Jack cheese

Garnish: sour cream

- Melt butter in a large saucepan over medium heat; add onion and garlic. Sauté until tender. Add broth and next 8 ingredients. Bring to a boil; cover, reduce heat, and simmer 20 to 30 minutes.

- Fry tortilla strips in hot oil in a skillet until crisp.

- Sprinkle tortilla strips and cheese evenly in individual soup bowls; ladle soup into each bowl. Garnish, if desired. Serve immediately.

Serves 6 to 8

Tortilla strips may also be baked until crisp.

Cheese melts more quickly and evenly when finely shredded. For ease in grating or shredding, work with well-chilled cheese.

Hearty Chili

2	pounds boneless beef chuck roast, cut into bite-size pieces
2	large onions, chopped
3	celery ribs, sliced into 1-inch pieces
1	large green bell pepper, chopped
1	large red bell pepper, chopped
2	jalapeño peppers, seeded and chopped
4	garlic cloves, minced
3	tablespoons olive oil
2	tablespoons cocoa
2	tablespoons chili powder
1	teaspoon ground cumin
1	teaspoon dried oregano
1	teaspoon paprika
1	teaspoon ground turmeric
½	teaspoon salt
½	teaspoon ground cardamom
¼	teaspoon ground black pepper
1	tablespoon molasses
½	cup dry red wine
2	(16-ounce) cans whole tomatoes, undrained and chopped or 2 cans diced tomatoes, undrained

- Cook first 7 ingredients in hot oil in a large Dutch oven over medium-high heat, stirring constantly, until meat is browned. Drain and return meat mixture to Dutch oven. Stir in cocoa and next 13 ingredients. Bring to a boil; cover, reduce heat, and simmer, stirring occasionally, 1½ hours.
- Serve chili with Sour Cream Topping and shredded cheese.

Yields 12 cups

(Hearty Chili continued)

1   (16-ounce) can kidney
    beans, drained
1   (16-ounce) can garbanzo
    beans, drained
    Sour Cream Topping
    Shredded sharp cheddar
    cheese

Sour Cream Topping

1   (8-ounce) container light
    sour cream

⅓   cup salsa

2   tablespoons light
    mayonnaise

1   teaspoon chili powder

½   teaspoon onion powder

½   teaspoon curry powder
    Dash of ground red
    pepper

1   tablespoon lemon juice

1   teaspoon Dijon mustard

• Combine all ingredients in a bowl;
chill.

Yields 1⅔ cups

*The coal eyes and buttons of a traditional snowperson can easily be replaced
with fruits and vegetables, such as radishes, carrots, cucumbers, apples,
and oranges. A discussion with the children of being a healthy snowperson
will soon follow, and the animals outdoors will appreciate the treats.*

Pizza Soup

5	(10½-ounce) cans minestrone soup
2½	cans water
1½-2	pounds Italian sausage, cooked, drained, and sliced
1	(10-ounce) package frozen spinach, thawed
1	(16-ounce) can tomatoes, undrained and chopped
1	teaspoon garlic salt
1	teaspoon dried oregano
	Grated Parmesan cheese
	Shredded mozzarella cheese

- Simmer first 7 ingredients in a large saucepan 30 minutes. Sprinkle with cheeses and serve.

Serves 8 to 10

Any bag of frozen vegetables can be a substitute for an ice pack in case of injury. It's a quick grab and shapes easily to the contour of the injury.

Old Town Alexandria Crab Soup

1   medium carrot, diced

1   small onion, diced

2   tablespoons vegetable
     oil

1   (14½-ounce) can whole
     tomatoes, undrained

1   (15-ounce) can lima
     beans

1   (14½-ounce) can corn

2   (10½-ounce) cans beef
     broth, undiluted

1   cup frozen or canned
     green beans

1   beef bouillon cube

4-5 teaspoons seafood
     seasoning

     Freshly ground pepper
     to taste

1   pound fresh lump
     crabmeat, drained

1   tablespoon dried parsley

- Sauté carrot and onion in hot oil
  in a large Dutch oven 10 minutes
  or until tender.

- Drain liquid from tomatoes,
  beans, and corn. Add broth and
  enough water to vegetable liquid
  to measure 2 quarts; add to Dutch
  oven.

- Chop tomatoes; add tomatoes,
  beans, and next 6 ingredients to
  soup. Cook, covered, over low
  heat 10 to 20 minutes.

- Stir crabmeat and parsley into
  soup and cook until thoroughly
  heated. Serve hot.

Serves 4 to 6

Alexandria was settled in the 1700s, largely by Scots. George Washington, who assisted in the early survey work, considered Alexandria his hometown. Today, many of the 18th- and 19th-century structures have been restored, making Old Town a vibrant urban community. You can stroll along Alexandria's waterfront and imagine great ships coming into port to load and unload.

Barley-Vegetable Soup

⅔ cup fine pearl barley, rinsed

11 cups brown stock or beef broth, divided

5 tablespoons butter or margarine, divided

1 onion, minced

2 carrots, peeled and chopped

2 celery ribs, chopped

2 potatoes, peeled and diced

1 (8-ounce) package fresh mushrooms, sliced

Pepper to taste

½ teaspoon ground thyme

3 tablespoons sour cream

Garnish: chopped fresh dill or parsley

- Bring barley and 3 cups stock to a boil in a large Dutch oven; reduce heat and simmer 1 hour, or until tender, adding water as needed to keep covered.

- Melt 3 tablespoons butter in a large skillet over medium heat; add onion and sauté until tender. Add carrots, celery, and potatoes; cover and cook 15 minutes or until tender. Add vegetables to Dutch oven.

- Melt remaining 2 tablespoons butter in skillet over medium heat; add mushrooms and sauté until browned. Add mushrooms to Dutch oven.

- Add remaining stock, pepper, and thyme to Dutch oven. Bring soup to a boil; reduce heat and simmer, stirring occasionally, 5 minutes.

- Combine sour cream and ½ cup soup in a small bowl, stirring until smooth; add to Dutch oven and bring almost to a boil. Serve immediately. Garnish, if desired.

Serves 8

Serve soup in your collection of tea cups and saucers on a silver tray. Your guests can drink their soup or use a spoon.

Burgundy Beef Stew

1	cup Burgundy or other dry red wine
1	(8-ounce) can tomato sauce
2	tablespoons red wine vinegar
3	garlic cloves, crushed
2	bay leaves
½	teaspoon freshly ground pepper
½	teaspoon ground allspice
1	pound stew beef, cut into 1-inch pieces
¼	cup olive oil
2	(10½-ounce) cans beef broth, undiluted
1	(9-ounce) package frozen green beans
1	medium onion, coarsely chopped
3	carrots, peeled and sliced
2	tablespoons all-purpose flour
2	tablespoons water

- Combine first 7 ingredients in a shallow dish, stirring well. Add beef; cover and chill at least 8 hours or overnight. Remove beef from marinade, reserving marinade. Remove and discard bay leaves.

- Brown beef in hot oil in a large Dutch oven over medium heat; drain and return beef to Dutch oven. Add reserved marinade and broth to beef and bring to a boil; cover, reduce heat, and simmer 1½ hours. Add green beans, onion, and carrots, stirring well. Cover and cook 30 minutes or until vegetables are tender.

- Combine flour and 2 tablespoons water, stirring until smooth; add to soup, stirring well. Cook until soup is thickened. Serve with crusty bread and a green salad.

Serves 3 to 4

𝒦eep olive oil from turning rancid by storing in the refrigerator. It hardens, but will liquefy quickly as it sits at room temperature.

Waterfront Gumbo

2 pounds unpeeled, medium-size fresh shrimp
1 cup vegetable oil
1 cup all-purpose flour
4 green onions, chopped
4 medium onions, chopped
2 large red bell peppers, seeded and chopped
2 celery ribs, sliced
5 garlic cloves, chopped
2 (14½-ounce) cans Italian-style tomatoes, undrained and chopped
2 (10½-ounce) packages frozen sliced okra, thawed
1 pound Polish sausage, sliced and cooked
1 (6-ounce) can tomato paste
2 quarts water
4 bay leaves
3 tablespoons lemon juice
2 teaspoons dried thyme
1 teaspoon salt
¾ teaspoon freshly ground black pepper
½ teaspoon Creole seasoning
½ teaspoon ground red pepper
1 pound fresh lump crabmeat, drained
3 tablespoons dried parsley
   Hot cooked white rice

- Peel shrimp and devein, if desired.
- Cook oil and flour in a large heavy Dutch oven over medium heat, stirring constantly, 10 to 15 minutes or until roux is chocolate-colored.
- Stir green onions and next 4 ingredients into roux; cook, stirring constantly, 3 to 5 minutes. Stir in tomatoes and next 11 ingredients; cover, reduce heat, and simmer, stirring occasionally, 1½ hours. Remove and discard bay leaves. Stir in seafood and parsley; simmer 5 to 10 minutes or until shrimp turn pink.
- Serve over hot cooked rice.

Serves 6 to 8

Roasted Garlic and Potato Soup

1	garlic bulb
1	teaspoon olive oil
1½	pounds Yukon gold potatoes, peeled and diced
1	large onion, chopped
2	large shallots, chopped
5	cups chicken broth
2	carrots, peeled and cut into large pieces
1	teaspoon salt
	Several fresh thyme and rosemary sprigs
1	cup light cream
1	cup skim milk
	Salt and freshly ground pepper to taste

- Preheat oven to 375°.

- Peel heavier pieces of skin from garlic bulb, leaving cloves and a small amount of skin intact. Sprinkle with oil and wrap in aluminum foil.

- Bake at 375° for 20 to 30 minutes or until cloves feel soft when squeezed.

- Remove from oven and let cool. Pull off cloves and gently squeeze pulp into a bowl.

- Bring potatoes and next 6 ingredients to a boil in a large Dutch oven; cover, reduce heat, and simmer 20 to 30 minutes or until carrot and potatoes are tender. Remove and discard herb sprigs.

- Coarsely mash potato mixture in Dutch oven using a potato masher. Cook 10 minutes or until soup is thickened. Stir in cream and milk; cook over medium-low heat until thoroughly heated. Season with salt and pepper to taste.

Serves 8

*H*int *for extra potatoes and onions: Cut up a few extra potatoes and onions, and process in a food processor a few seconds. They will make potato patties to fry with your next breakfast or brunch.*

Hunt Club Corn Chowder

3	potatoes, peeled and cut into 1-inch pieces
2	sweet potatoes, peeled and cut into 1-inch pieces
2	tablespoons minced garlic
⅓	cup chopped celery
3	cups diced onion
2	tablespoons olive oil
1	red bell pepper, seeded and diced
1	green bell pepper, seeded and diced
⅓	cup canned green chiles, coarsely chopped
¼	cup white wine
½	tablespoon dried oregano
½	tablespoon dried basil
2	teaspoons ground cumin
2	cups drained canned corn kernels
1	tablespoon salt
1	tablespoon coarsely ground black pepper
½	cup fresh cilantro, chopped
	Baked Tortilla Chips (recipe on page 119)

- In a large Dutch oven, cover potatoes with water and bring to a boil; reduce heat and simmer for 10 minutes. Drain.

- Sauté garlic, celery, and onion in hot oil in a large saucepan until tender; add bell peppers and chiles. Add white wine and cook, stirring to loosen browned particles. Add oregano, basil, and cumin, stirring well.

- Add potatoes and enough water to cover vegetables by 2 inches. Bring to a boil, and cook another 10 minutes or until potatoes are "fork-tender" (do not overcook). Stir in corn, salt, and pepper. Cook just until thoroughly heated. Remove from heat and stir in cilantro.

- Serve with Baked Tortilla Chips for a great low-fat meal.

Serves 8 to 10

(Hunt Club Corn Chowder continued)

Baked Tortilla Chips

1   package flour tortillas
Vegetable cooking spray
Crab seasoning,
    seasoned salt, ground
    cumin, chili powder,
    garlic powder, or
    onion powder

• Cut tortillas into eighths and place in a single layer on baking sheets. Coat lightly with vegetable cooking spray and sprinkle with desired seasonings. Bake at 400° for 10 minutes.

Coconut-Chicken Soup

2	(14-ounce) cans unsweetened coconut milk
8	cups chicken broth
¼	cup white wine
¾	cup fresh lemon grass, sliced into ¼-inch-thick pieces
2	bone-in chicken breasts
3	tablespoons lime juice
1	jalapeño pepper, chopped
1	tablespoon jalapeño pepper juice (from jar)
	Finely chopped fresh cilantro

- Bring first 4 ingredients to a boil in a large saucepan. Add chicken; reduce heat and simmer, turning occasionally, 15 minutes or until chicken is almost done.

- Transfer chicken to a plate and let cool. Remove skin and bones from chicken and cut into ½-inch pieces.

- Pour soup through a wire-mesh strainer, discarding solids. Return soup to saucepan; add lime juice, jalapeño pepper, and jalapeño juice. Simmer 30 minutes.

- Add chicken to soup and simmer until thoroughly heated. Adjust seasonings to taste, adding more lime juice if desired.

- Ladle into bowls and sprinkle with cilantro. Serve immediately.

Serves 6

Try this Thai-style dish for a South Pacific-style party.

One Dish
Meals

Quick but Elegant

Creamy Tomato-Sausage
Sauce with Shells, *page 134*

Green Salad with
Summer Tomato Dressing, *page 231*

Refrigerator Rolls, *page 163*

Cherry Butter Cake, *page 266*

Life On The Run

Friends are coming for dinner after work, and the Beltway's backed up again. Don't worry, your friends are stuck in traffic too! You need to stop by the dry cleaners to pick up your black suit for tomorrow's big presentation, the grocery store for fresh chicken and tomatoes, and oh yes, you have to pick up the children from piano lessons and soccer practice. Finally you are home with ten minutes to throw together that company dinner.

Whether you are juggling long hours at the office, attending graduate school, trying to fit in a social life, constantly carpooling the children, or just trying to be all things to all people, there is never enough time in our lives. And remember, you promised yourself you would not order pizza this week! Now you can understand why our lives are constantly on the run.

If you see yourself here, then let our collection of one-dish meals provide you inspiration. All cooks need a few little secrets to help pull off the impossible when it seems impossible to do! So the next time you want to invite those friends over for dinner after work, or if you are invited at the last minute for a pot-luck, just smile and say, "I'd love to, but *What Can I Bring?*" and duck into this section for some great ideas.

Tomato-Basil Vinaigrette for Pasta

8   medium-size vine-
      ripened tomatoes,
      seeded and finely
      chopped

2   tablespoons minced
      shallots

1   tablespoon minced
      garlic

2-3 fresh basil sprigs,
      chopped

¼   cup fresh lemon juice
      (2-3 lemons)

1   cup virgin olive oil

6   tablespoons finely
      chopped fresh parsley,
      divided

      Freshly ground pepper
      to taste

• Combine first 6 ingredients and
  4 tablespoons parsley. Add
  pepper to taste. Let sit at room
  temperature 15 to 20 minutes, if
  desired.

• Transfer mixture to a medium
  saucepan; cook over low heat
  5 minutes or until warm.

• Serve over hot cooked pasta
  and sprinkle with remaining
  2 tablespoons parsley.

Serves 6

*This is a fresh and light accompani-
ment. It's good over ravioli.*

Pasta with Sausage, Leeks, and Mushrooms

1	pound garlic sausage
¼	cup unsalted butter
1	leek, white and firm green parts sliced
4	green onions, chopped
1	pound fresh mushrooms, quartered
¼	cup white wine
½	cup fresh parsley, minced
1	pound egg fettuccine, cooked
½	cup fat-free ricotta cheese

- Brown sausage in a skillet over medium heat; slice into ½-inch pieces and return to skillet. Cook until done; cover and set aside.

- Melt butter in a large saucepan over medium heat; add leek, green onions, and mushrooms. Sauté until tender. Add wine and cook until most of liquid is evaporated. Stir in parsley.

- Place hot cooked pasta in a large serving bowl; add ricotta, tossing well. Add vegetable mixture, tossing well. Add sausage, tossing well. Serve immediately.

Serves 4

Follow Mother Nature's lead in deciding whether to cook vegetables covered or uncovered. Cover those vegetables that are covered by nature, i.e. those that grow underground, and leave those that grow above ground uncovered.

Pasta with Prosciutto

1	medium onion, finely chopped
2	celery ribs, finely chopped
4	garlic cloves, minced
¼	cup olive oil
½	pound thinly sliced prosciutto, finely chopped
¾	cup vodka
1	(28-ounce) can crushed tomatoes
¼	teaspoon ground red pepper
2	tablespoons chopped fresh parsley
2	tablespoons dried basil, crushed
1	teaspoon dried oregano, crushed
1	cup half-and-half
1	pound pasta, cooked

- Sauté first 3 ingredients in hot oil in a large skillet, stirring often, until tender. Add prosciutto and vodka; reduce heat and simmer 5 minutes or until liquid is evaporated. Add tomatoes and next 4 ingredients; simmer 10 minutes. Stir in half-and-half and simmer 3 to 4 minutes.

- Toss together hot cooked pasta and sauce; serve immediately.

Serves 4 to 6

Include food scissors in your gadget drawer. They come in handy for snipping or chopping fresh herbs. Just run them through the dishwasher to clean.

Three-Cheese Ravioli

1   (9-ounce) package fresh
     or frozen cheese-filled
     ravioli
1   (14½-ounce) can
     tomatoes, chopped
¼   cup chopped onion
1   garlic clove, chopped
1   teaspoon dried or
     1 tablespoon chopped
     fresh basil
½   cup sliced fresh
     mushrooms
¼   cup red cooking wine
⅛   teaspoon salt
⅛   teaspoon pepper
½   cup cottage or ricotta
     cheese
2   tablespoons grated
     Parmesan cheese

- Preheat oven to 350°.
- Cook ravioli according to package directions.
- Puree tomatoes and next 3 ingredients in a food processor; combine mixture with mushrooms and next 3 ingredients in a skillet. Cook over medium-high heat, stirring often, 5 minutes or until liquid has evaporated.
- Place ravioli in a 10 x 6 x 2-inch baking dish; spread cottage cheese over ravioli. Pour tomato sauce over cottage cheese. Sprinkle with Parmesan cheese.
- Bake at 350° for 20 minutes or until thoroughly heated.

Serves 4

*M*ushrooms will stay fresh longer if left unwashed and stored in paper or damp cloth bags until ready to use.

Bow-Tie Pasta with Asparagus in Lemon Cream Sauce

3   garlic cloves, minced

1   pound asparagus, peeled and cut into ½-inch pieces

1   tablespoon olive oil

2   tablespoons fresh lemon juice

½   cup heavy cream

½   cup milk

    Zest of 1 lemon

¼   teaspoon ground nutmeg

¼   teaspoon salt

¼   teaspoon pepper

1   pound bow-tie pasta, cooked

⅓   cup grated Parmesan cheese

- Sauté garlic and asparagus in hot oil in a large nonstick skillet, stirring constantly, 2 minutes. Stir in lemon juice; cover and cook 5 minutes or until asparagus is tender.

- Combine cream and next 5 ingredients; pour over asparagus and bring to a boil.

- Combine hot cooked pasta and asparagus mixture in a large serving bowl, tossing to coat. Stir in Parmesan cheese and serve immediately.

Serves 4 to 6

Choose asparagus stalks that are tender and firm with tips that are close and compact. The most tender stalks show very little white anywhere. Fresh asparagus must be used immediately because it will get tough quickly.

White Lasagna

1½ pounds ground pork sausage or beef
1   cup chopped onion
½   cup chopped celery
2   garlic cloves, minced
2   teaspoons dried basil
1   teaspoon dried oregano
½   teaspoon dried Italian seasoning
½   teaspoon salt
1   cup half-and-half
1   (3-ounce) package cream cheese
½   cup white cooking wine
2   cups (8 ounces) shredded cheddar cheese
1½ cups (6 ounces) shredded Gouda cheese
1   (12-ounce) container cottage cheese
1   large egg
8   lasagna noodles, cooked
2   cups (8 ounces) shredded mozzarella cheese

- Cook first 4 ingredients in a skillet over medium heat, stirring until sausage is crumbled and no longer pink. Stir in basil and next 5 ingredients. Stir in wine, cheddar cheese, and Gouda cheese; cook, stirring constantly, until cheese is melted. Set aside.

- Combine cottage cheese and egg.

- Arrange half of noodles in a 9 x 13 x 2-inch baking dish; layer with half each of meat mixture, cottage cheese mixture, and mozzarella cheese. Repeat layers once.

- Bake at 350° for 40 minutes. Let stand at room temperature 10 minutes before serving.

Serves 6 to 8

How can I travel with a casserole? Place your casserole dish in a box, and wrap a towel around it. The towel will absorb spills and keep the dish warm in transit.

Key Lime Pasta with Black Beans

7	garlic cloves, chopped
¼	cup olive oil
⅔	cup fresh Key lime juice
½	cup dry sherry
2	cups chopped green onions
1	pound plum tomatoes, chopped
2	(15-ounce) cans black beans, rinsed and drained
1	teaspoon salt
½	teaspoon ground black pepper
1½	tablespoons grated lime rind
12	ounces bow-tie pasta, cooked
½	cup chopped fresh Italian parsley

- Sauté garlic in hot oil in a skillet until tender. Add lime juice and sherry and cook over high heat 5 minutes or until reduced to ¼ cup. Add green onions and tomato; cook over medium heat, stirring occasionally 5 to 8 minutes. Stir in black beans and next 3 ingredients.

- Combine hot cooked pasta and sauce in a large serving bowl, tossing to coat. Sprinkle with parsley and serve immediately.

Serves 8

This is a very colorful presentation for a family main dish or as a side dish for a party. It also gets "better with age."

Creamy Salmon Fettuccine

1 cup fresh or frozen baby green peas

1½ pounds fresh or dried spinach, tomato, or plain fettuccine, cooked

1 tablespoon olive oil

½ pound smoked salmon, thinly sliced into 1-inch strips and divided

1 pint heavy cream or milk, divided

1 tablespoon minced shallots

2 tablespoons white wine

Salt and pepper to taste

- Cook fresh peas in boiling water to cover 3 minutes or frozen peas according to package directions; drain and rinse with cold water; set aside.

- Combine hot cooked pasta and oil in a large serving bowl, tossing to coat; set aside.

- Puree one-third of the salmon, 2 tablespoons heavy cream, and shallots in a blender or food processor until smooth and creamy.

- Bring wine to a boil in a small saucepan; add remaining heavy cream and cook, stirring constantly, until smooth. Reduce heat to low; add salmon mixture, stirring well. Cook over low heat, stirring constantly, until thoroughly heated. Salt and pepper to taste.

- Add remaining salmon and peas to pasta, tossing well. Pour hot sauce over mixture, tossing to coat. Serve immediately.

Serves 4

Potomac Pork Pasta

1   pound boneless pork loin, cut into 1-inch cubes

½   teaspoon vegetable oil

¼   cup chopped yellow onion

¼   cup seeded and chopped green bell pepper

¼   cup seeded and chopped red bell pepper

1   (14½-ounce) can diced tomatoes

1   teaspoon dried Italian seasoning

1   teaspoon dried basil

¼   teaspoon ground black pepper

¼   teaspoon salt

⅛   teaspoon ground red pepper

3   cups wide egg noodles, cooked

- Brown pork on all sides in hot oil in a skillet over medium heat; add onion and bell pepper. Stir-fry until meat is done. Stir in tomatoes and next 5 ingredients. Cover, reduce heat, and simmer 10 minutes.

- Arrange hot cooked noodles on a serving platter; cover with pork sauce.

Serves 4

It is important that the vegetables are cut the same size so they cook the same-not some mushy and others crisp.

Chilled Tortellini Salad

¾ cup olive oil

½ cup white wine vinegar

½ teaspoon black pepper

2 garlic cloves, minced

1 teaspoon chili powder

1 teaspoon dry mustard

1 teaspoon paprika

1 teaspoon ground cumin

1 teaspoon salt

Dash of hot sauce

1 cup seeded and diced green bell pepper

1 cup diced purple onion

2 cups chopped tomato

½ cup parsley, minced

6 tablespoons spicy barbecue sauce

1 pound cheese tortellini, cooked

Shredded lettuce

½ cup (2 ounces) shredded cheddar cheese

- Combine first 15 ingredients in a large bowl; add cooked tortellini, tossing well. Chill 2 to 4 hours.

- Place shredded lettuce on a serving platter; top with pasta mixture and sprinkle with cheddar cheese.

Serves 6

When bringing a cold dish to a gathering, freeze a stoneware bowl ahead of time. Before departing, transfer food into the frozen bowl, and cover with aluminum foil. The food will stay cool while in transit and longer once you arrive.

Grilled Eggplant and Goat Cheese Salad

½ cup olive oil

½ cup chopped fresh basil

¼ cup red wine vinegar

3 teaspoons brown sugar

2 teaspoons salt

½ teaspoon pepper

1 medium eggplant
(1 to 1½ pounds)

1 cup crumbled goat or
feta cheese

8 cups gourmet salad
greens

1 cup diced fresh tomato

- Whisk together first 6 ingredients; pour half of mixture into a 9 x 13 x 2-inch baking dish, reserving remainder.

- Slice eggplant crosswise into ½-inch thick slices; add to baking dish, turning to coat. Let stand at room temperature 15 to 20 minutes. Remove eggplant from marinade, reserving marinade.

- Grill eggplant over medium heat (350° to 375°), basting with reserved marinade, 5 to 8 minutes on each side or until tender and golden. Sprinkle with goat cheese and grill 1 to 2 more minutes or until cheese is softened.

- Combine reserved dressing and salad greens, tossing to coat. Arrange lettuce on 4 serving plates; top evenly with eggplant slices, overlapping slices slightly. Sprinkle with diced tomato and serve immediately.

Serves 4

Clifton Day Pasta

1 pound dried fettuccine

6 garlic cloves, chopped

2 tablespoons extra-virgin olive oil

1 pound fresh button mushrooms, sliced

2 cans artichoke hearts, quartered with juice reserved

Salt and freshly cracked pepper to taste

2 cups chicken stock

¼ cup dry white wine

1-2 cups cooked chicken or shrimp (optional)

½-¾ cup Italian-seasoned breadcrumbs

½ cup butter or margarine, melted

⅓ cup grated Parmesan and Romano cheeses

Garnishes: lemon slices, fresh parsley sprigs

• Preheat oven to 325°. Cook pasta in boiling water to cover until al dente. Drain and rinse with cold water; set aside.

• Cook garlic in hot oil in a saucepan over medium heat, stirring constantly, 20 seconds. Add mushrooms and artichoke hearts. Cook 1 to 2 minutes. Add salt and pepper to taste.

• Combine chicken stock and artichoke juice in a 9 x 13 x 2-inch baking dish; stir in wine. Add pasta, spreading evenly across bottom of pan. Sprinkle evenly with chicken, if desired. Cover with mushroom mixture.

• Bake at 325° for 12 minutes. Remove from oven and sprinkle with breadcrumbs; drizzle with butter.

• Broil until breadcrumbs are brown and crisp. Sprinkle with cheeses, and garnish, if desired.

Serves 8

This delicious dish is best if made the night before. It's a great casserole to take to a sick friend or someone with a new baby because it can be frozen in zip-top plastic freezer bags after it has been cooked. Simply thaw and reheat to enjoy at your convenience.

Creamy Tomato-Sausage Sauce with Shells

1   pound hot or mild Italian pork sausage links

3   tablespoons butter or margarine

1   teaspoon finely chopped fresh or dried rosemary

1½ pounds fresh plum tomatoes, chopped into ½-inch pieces, or 1 (28-ounce) can diced tomatoes

3   tablespoons water

    Dried red pepper flakes to taste

    Salt to taste

¾   cup heavy cream

    Hot cooked pasta shells

½   cup grated Parmigiano-Reggiano cheese

- Boil sausage links in water to cover 3 to 4 minutes; let cool and slice into thin rounds.

- Melt butter in a skillet over medium-high heat; add sausage, cook until lightly browned. Add rosemary, tomato, and 3 tablespoons water; cook 7 to 10 minutes or until water is evaporated and tomato forms a sauce. Add red pepper flakes and salt to taste. Gradually add cream and cook, stirring often, until cream is reduced by half and sauce is creamy.

- Remove skillet from heat. Add hot cooked pasta shells and cheese to sauce, tossing to coat. Serve immediately.

Serves 6

This mouth watering dish is best if eaten soon after cooking. Serve with a dry red wine, garlic bread, and a green salad.

Tortilla-Black Bean Casserole

2 cups chopped onion

4 cups seeded and chopped green and/or red bell pepper

1 (14½-ounce) can tomatoes, undrained

1 cup salsa

2 garlic cloves, minced

2 teaspoons ground cumin

2 (15-ounce) cans black beans, drained

12 (6-inch) corn tortillas

3 cups (12 ounces) shredded Monterey Jack cheese

- Simmer first 6 ingredients in a skillet; add black beans and simmer until thoroughly heated.

- Layer one-third each of bean mixture, tortillas, and cheese in a 9 x 13 x 2-inch baking dish; repeat layers twice.

- Bake at 350° for 30 to 35 minutes.

Serves 8

"Always a crowd pleaser" has been heard frequently about this dish. One of the benefits is that it can be made as spicy or as mild as you desire.

Pulled Beef Sandwiches

1   tablespoon butter or margarine

2   tablespoons olive oil

1   (3- to 4-pound) bottom round beef roast, trimmed

Salt and pepper to taste

2   cups beef stock

3   cups red wine (Burgundy or Chianti), divided

8   crusty rolls

Simmered Onions (recipe on page 137)

¼   cup minced fresh parsley

- Melt butter and oil in a large Dutch oven over medium heat. Rub roast with salt and pepper to taste.

- Brown roast in Dutch oven. Add beef stock and 1 cup wine. Cover and simmer 4 to 5 hours or until meat is easily shredded with a fork, adding ½ cup wine each hour.

- Transfer roast to a platter, reserving drippings in pan; let cool to room temperature. Shred beef using two forks; return shredded beef to drippings.

- Serve immediately on crusty rolls with Simmered Onions and parsley or chill several days.

Serves 8 to 10

(Pulled Beef Sandwiches continued)

Simmered Onions

½   cup butter or margarine

10   cups ¼-inch-thick
       yellow onion slices
       (4 to 5 large onions)

1   cup dry red wine

¾   cup red wine vinegar

⅓   cup sugar
      Salt and pepper to taste

- Melt butter in a saucepan over medium heat; add onions and remaining ingredients. Cover, reduce heat, and simmer 1 hour. Uncover and simmer 2 more hours.

- Serve immediately with beef or chill up to 2 days. Reheat to serve.

To serve: Heat beef and juices in pan on top of stove or microwave. Place pulled beef on sandwich roll or toast. Top with a bit of minced parsley and pan juices. It's also good with sautéed onions.

This is a wonderful fall or winter weekend casual lunch or supper meal. Perfect to make a day or two in advance.

Sausage and Roasted Vegetable Couscous

1	pound spicy turkey sausage
6	carrots, peeled and sliced in 1-inch pieces
4	red potatoes, quartered
2	fennel bulbs, quartered
4	tablespoons vegetable oil, divided
2	tablespoons coarse-grained sea salt, divided
1	pound asparagus
1	yellow onion, quartered
2	cups couscous
2½	cups water

- Preheat oven to 450°.

- Brown sausage in a skillet over medium heat; cut into ½-inch slices and cook until done. Cover and set aside.

- Place carrots, potato, and fennel in a 9 x 13 x 2-inch baking dish; add 2 tablespoons oil and 1 tablespoon salt, tossing to coat.

- Bake at 450° for 20 minutes, stirring after 10 minutes.

- Combine asparagus, onion, remaining 2 tablespoons oil, and remaining 1 tablespoon salt in a separate baking dish, tossing to coat.

- Bake at 450° for 15 minutes.

- Prepare couscous according to package directions.

- Spoon couscous into a serving bowl; surround with roasted vegetables and top with sliced sausage.

Serves 6

Fabulous Fajitas

1½ pounds beef sirloin steak, flank steak, or chicken

¼ cup olive oil

¼ cup balsamic vinegar

1 teaspoon sugar

1 tablespoon chopped fresh oregano

1 teaspoon chili powder

1 garlic clove, minced

2 tablespoons chopped onion

½ teaspoon salt

½ teaspoon pepper

Tortillas

Toppings: guacamole, pico de gallo, shredded Monterey Jack cheese, sliced onion, and sour cream

- Prick meat all over with a fork. Combine meat and next 9 ingredients. Chill 8 to 24 hours. Remove meat from marinade, discarding marinade.

- Grill meat over medium-high heat (375° to 400°) 8 minutes on each side or until desired degree of doneness. Cut meat across the grain into thin strips.

- Serve with warm tortillas and desired toppings.

Serves 4

A sort of relish, pico de gallo is a mixture of chopped ingredients — usually green bell peppers, onions, cucumbers, and others — and assorted seasonings. It can be found in the international foods sections of larger supermarkets and in Latin American neighborhood grocery stores.

Veggie and Bean Quesadillas

¼ cup chopped fresh or frozen red or green bell pepper

¾ cup chopped fresh or frozen onion

½ cup diced fresh or frozen carrots

3 tablespoons olive oil, divided

1 small yellow squash, sliced

1 small zucchini, sliced

1 cup chopped fresh or frozen broccoli

¼ cup frozen corn kernels

¼ cup frozen green peas

½ teaspoon garlic powder

½ teaspoon chili powder

½ teaspoon ground rubbed sage

½ teaspoon ground cumin

Salt and freshly ground pepper to taste

1 (16-ounce) can refried black or pinto beans

4 soft flour tortillas

¾-1 cup (3 to 4 ounces) shredded regular or low-fat Monterey Jack cheese

1 cup salsa

1 cup sour cream (optional)

- Sauté first 3 ingredients in 2 tablespoons hot oil in a large skillet, stirring occasionally, 10 minutes or until tender. Add squash and next 9 ingredients; cook, stirring occasionally, 15 minutes or until desired degree of doneness (do not overcook). Set aside, uncovered, 1 to 2 hours, if desired.

- Heat beans according to package directions.

- If vegetables have been set aside; microwave at MEDIUM (50% power) 1 minute to reheat.

- Place 1 tortilla in a small amount of hot oil in a separate large skillet; spread one-fourth each of beans, vegetable mixture, and cheese over half of tortilla. Fold tortilla in half. Cook 2 to 3 minutes on each side. Repeat process with remaining tortillas, beans, vegetable mixture, and cheese.

- Serve immediately with salsa and sour cream, if desired.

Serves 2 to 4

For a Curry Quesadilla, substitute coriander and turmeric for chili powder and sage, and cooked lentils for refried beans. Top with mango chutney instead of salsa and sour cream.

This recipe is very flexible. You can use whatever vegetables you like or may have on hand-fresh or frozen.

Zucchini Enchiladas

1   dozen large corn
      tortillas
      Vegetable oil
1   pound lean ground beef
1   yellow onion, minced
2   tablespoons vegetable
      oil
4   cups grated zucchini
1   small can green or ripe
      olives, drained and
      chopped
2   teaspoons crushed
      garlic
1   tablespoon ground
      cumin
      Salt and pepper to taste
2½-3 cups (10 to 12 ounces)
      shredded Monterey
      Jack cheese, divided
3   (7-ounce) cans
      commercial enchilada
      sauce

- Fry tortillas in hot oil 2 minutes
  (they should still be pliable); drain
  on paper towels.

- Cook beef and onion in
  2 tablespoons hot oil in a skillet
  over medium heat 10 minutes;
  drain. Add zucchini and next
  4 ingredients to beef mixture;
  cook 5 minutes. Add 2 cups
  cheese, stirring well.

- Spoon beef mixture evenly on
  tortillas; roll up tortillas, and place
  seam side down in a 9 x 13 x 2-inch
  baking dish. Pour enchilada sauce
  over top and sprinkle with remaining cheese.

- Bake at 350° for 15 minutes.

Serves 8

*Prepared enchiladas may be refriger-
ated before baking. Increase baking
time to 30 minutes.*

Black Bean Enchiladas

1¼ cups finely chopped onion

2 garlic cloves, minced

2 (15-ounce) cans black beans, rinsed and drained

1 tablespoon lime juice

½ teaspoon dried oregano

¼ teaspoon salt

½ cup sour cream

1 tablespoon plus 1 teaspoon minced fresh cilantro

8 (6-inch) corn tortillas

Enchilada Sauce

1 cup (4 ounces) shredded taco blend cheese

- Sauté onion and garlic in a nonstick skillet coated with vegetable cooking spray over medium-high heat until tender. Mash 1 can of beans and add both cans and next 3 ingredients to skillet, stirring well. Set aside.

- Stir together sour cream and cilantro.

- Bake tortillas wrapped in aluminum foil at 325° for 12 minutes or until thoroughly heated. Spread 1 tablespoon sour cream mixture over 1 side of each tortilla; spoon bean mixture evenly down center of tortillas. Loosely roll up tortillas.

- Spread ¾ cup Enchilada Sauce in a 9 x 13 x 2-inch baking dish coated with vegetable cooking spray. Arrange tortillas, seam side down, over sauce; top with remaining sauce.

- Bake, covered, at 350° for 15 minutes. Sprinkle evenly with cheese. Bake, uncovered, 5 more minutes.

(Black Bean Enchiladas continued)

Enchilada Sauce

1½ tablespoons butter or margarine

2 garlic cloves

2 tablespoons all-purpose flour

2 cups water

½ cup tomato sauce

1 tablespoon chili powder

¼ teaspoon salt

⅛ teaspoon dried whole oregano

⅛ teaspoon ground cumin

- Melt butter in a saucepan coated with vegetable cooking spray over medium heat; add garlic and sauté until tender.

- Combine flour and next 6 ingredients, stirring until smooth; add to garlic and bring to a boil, stirring constantly. Reduce heat, and simmer, stirring constantly, 15 minutes. Serve warm.

Serves 4 to 6

Spicy Tortilla Casserole

1¼ pounds ground turkey
or beef

1 onion, chopped

1 garlic clove, minced

1 tablespoon ground
cumin

1 teaspoon salt

1 (10-ounce) can mild
enchilada sauce

4 large flour tortillas

2 cups (8 ounces)
shredded cheddar and
Monterey Jack cheeses

1 (4-ounce) can mild green
chiles, drained and
chopped

½ teaspoon dried cilantro

Toppings: salsa, sour
cream

- Preheat oven to 350°.

- Brown turkey or beef in a large
skillet over medium heat, stirring
until it crumbles and is no longer
pink; drain. Add onion and next
4 ingredients to skillet; reduce
heat and simmer 5 to 10 minutes
or until onion is tender.

- Place 1 tortilla in the bottom of an
8- or 9-inch square baking dish
lightly coated with vegetable
cooking spray. Layer with one-
third of meat mixture, one-fourth
of cheeses, and one-third of green
chiles. Repeat layers twice. Top
with remaining tortilla. Sprinkle
with remaining cheese and
cilantro.

- Bake, covered, at 350° for
30 minutes. Uncover and bake
5 more minutes or until cheese is
melted.

- Let stand at room temperature
5 minutes before serving. Serve
with desired toppings.

Serves 4 to 6

Calico Bean Casserole

½   pound ground beef

½   pound chopped bacon

1   cup chopped onion

½   cup ketchup

1   teaspoon salt

2-4   drops Liquid Smoke

¾   cup brown sugar

1   teaspoon dry mustard

2   teaspoons vinegar

½   cup granulated sugar (optional)

2   pounds canned pork and beans, undrained

1   (14½-ounce) can butter beans, drained

1   (14½-ounce) can kidney beans, drained

- Cook first 3 ingredients in a saucepan over medium heat 10 minutes or until beef is crumbled and no longer pink and onion is tender; drain. Add ketchup, next 5 ingredients, and if desired, granulated sugar, stirring well.

- Place beans in a deep baking dish, and top with meat mixture.

- Bake at 300° for 1 hour and 15 minutes.

Serves 10

*U*se a purple onion to add extra color to this favorite.

Virginia Bicentennial Chicken Salad

¾ cup mayonnaise

1 teaspoon curry powder

2 teaspoons lemon juice

2 teaspoons soy sauce

2 cups cooked cubed chicken breast

1 (8-ounce) can sliced water chestnuts, drained

½ pound seedless green grapes, halved

1 (8-ounce) can pineapple tidbits, drained

½ cup chopped celery

½ cup slivered almonds, toasted

- Combine first 4 ingredients in a small bowl.

- Combine chicken and next 5 ingredients in a separate bowl; pour dressing over mixture, tossing to coat. Cover and chill overnight.

Serves 4

This salad was served to Queen Elizabeth when she visited the University of Virginia in 1976.

From our shore to mountains, the Commonwealth of Virginia has been called home by many for more than four centuries. It is the cradle to several of the founding fathers of our great nation. Because of Virginia's rich heritage and tradition, those who call it home-whether born or transplanted-feel the spirit, pride, history, and progress we as a community give.

Chilled Oriental Beef Salad

4   tablespoons lite soy
    sauce

3   tablespoons lime juice

2   teaspoons brown sugar

3   garlic cloves, chopped

1   (1-pound) boneless beef
    sirloin steak

2   tablespoons vegetable
    oil

2   heads leaf lettuce, torn

2   tablespoons chopped
    cilantro

2   tablespoons chopped
    roasted peanuts

- Combine first 4 ingredients,
  stirring until sugar dissolves.

- Place steak in a heavy-duty zip-
  top plastic bag. Set aside ¼ cup
  dressing and pour remaining
  dressing over steak. Seal, pressing
  out air, and chill 30 minutes,
  turning occasionally.

- Combine reserved ¼ cup dressing
  and oil in a jar; cover tightly and
  shake vigorously.

- Toss together lettuce and cilantro;
  chill.

- Remove steak from marinade,
  discarding marinade. Broil steak to
  desired degree of doneness. Cut
  across the grain into thin slices.

- Shake dressing and pour over
  greens, tossing to coat.

- Place greens on a large serving
  platter. Arrange steak slices over
  greens and sprinkle with peanuts.

Serves 4

If you have a guest who cannot eat nuts or if you simply don't have any in the cupboard, substitute the same amount of chopped water chestnuts or celery.

Vegetable Stir-Fry with Ginger Sauce

2   carrots, thinly sliced diagonally

1   onion, thinly sliced

1   red bell pepper, seeded and thinly sliced

2   garlic cloves, minced

3   tablespoons peanut oil

4   stalks bok choy, sliced

2   cups sliced Napa cabbage

1½   cups broccoli flowerets

1   cup frozen green peas

1   (8-ounce) can bamboo shoots, drained and rinsed

Dash of sesame oil

Ginger Sauce

½   pound firm tofu, cut into ½-inch cubes

3-4 cups hot cooked brown rice

Garnishes: toasted sesame seeds, chopped green onions

- Stir-fry first 4 ingredients in hot peanut oil in a wok or large skillet 3 to 4 minutes. Add bok choy and next 4 ingredients. Stir-fry 4 to 5 minutes or until vegetables are thoroughly heated and crisp-tender. Add sesame oil and half of Ginger Sauce. Gently stir in tofu; cover, reduce heat, and simmer 1 minute.

- Serve over hot cooked rice with remaining half of sauce; garnish, if desired.

(Vegetable Stir-Fry with Ginger Sauce continued)

Ginger Sauce

6	tablespoons rice vinegar
6	tablespoons sugar
¾	cup water
1½	tablespoons soy sauce
1	tablespoon water
1	tablespoon cornstarch
2	teaspoons minced fresh ginger

- Bring first 4 ingredients to a boil in a small saucepan; reduce heat, and simmer, stirring occasionally, 5 minutes.

- Combine 1 tablespoon water and cornstarch and stir into sauce. Cook, stirring occasionally, until clear and thickened. Remove from heat and stir in ginger.

- Chill up to 2 days, if desired. Reheat to serve.

Serves 4

Spinach and Feta Pizza

1   cup onion, chopped

3   garlic cloves, crushed

¼   teaspoon salt

2   tablespoons olive oil

½   teaspoon dried basil, crushed

½   teaspoon dried oregano

    Juice from half of a large lemon

1   pound fresh or 1 (10-ounce) package frozen spinach

½   cup butter or margarine, melted

¼   cup olive oil

½   pound phyllo pastry sheets

1   pound mozzarella cheese, shredded

1½ cups feta cheese, crumbled

2   tomatoes, sliced (optional)

½   cup breadcrumbs (optional)

- Sauté first 3 ingredients in 2 tablespoons hot oil in a large skillet until tender. Add basil and next 3 ingredients. Cook until spinach is limp and liquid is evaporated.

- Combine melted butter and ¼ cup oil.

- Layer phyllo sheets on a large heavily greased baking sheet, brushing each sheet generously with butter mixture. Spread spinach mixture over phyllo stack and top with mozzarella and feta cheese. Sprinkle with tomato and breadcrumbs, if desired.

- Bake at 400° for 25 to 30 minutes.

Serves 4 to 6

Green Chile Lasagna

1	(16-ounce) jar mild salsa
1	(16-ounce) jar medium salsa
¼	teaspoon ground black pepper
1-1½	tablespoons chili powder
1	teaspoon ground cumin
2	garlic cloves, minced
2	cups cottage cheese
2	large eggs
⅓	cup chopped fresh parsley
1	(4.5-ounce) can diced green chiles
1	(8-ounce) oven-ready lasagna
4	cups cubed cooked chicken
1	cup (4 ounces) shredded sharp cheddar cheese
1	cup (4 ounces) shredded Monterey Jack cheese

- Preheat oven to 375°.
- Bring first 6 ingredients to a boil in a non-aluminum saucepan. Reduce heat and simmer, stirring often, 10 minutes or until reduced to 4 cups.
- Combine cottage cheese and next 3 ingredients, stirring well.
- Arrange lasagna in a 9 x 13 x 2-inch baking dish lightly coated with vegetable cooking spray (do not overlap). Layer half each of cottage cheese mixture, chicken, and salsa mixture on top. Sprinkle with half of shredded cheeses. Repeat layers, ending with cheese.
- Bake, covered, at 375° for 45 to 50 minutes or until bubbly.
- Uncover and let stand at room temperature 10 minutes before serving.

Serves 8

Couscous Amandine

½   cup raisins

1   package couscous

½   teaspoon ground cinnamon

¼   cup chopped fresh parsley

2   tablespoons olive oil

⅓-½ cup slivered almonds, toasted

- Boil water to serve 6 for couscous; add raisins to plump. Add couscous and cook according to package directions.

- Stir in cinnamon, parsley, and oil. Add almonds just before serving.

Serves 8 to 10

Complement your meal with this dish instead of traditional rice.

Breads
and Brunches

Sumptuous Brunch

Strawberries Excellent, page 179

Hospitality Casserole, page 180

Sausage and Salsa Casserole, page 171

Asparagus with
Mustard-Yogurt Sauce, page 187

Orange-Poppy Seed Bread, page 154

Almond Pound Cake, page 265

Bride's Punch, page 42

Springtime Brings . . . House Guests!

Springtime in Northern Virginia! It's one of our favorite times of year. The region is ablaze with seasonal color, from the fields of daffodils that grace the George Washington Parkway to the cherry blossoms ringing the Tidal Basin downtown to the glorious azaleas and dogwoods that light up the wooded neighborhoods of Alexandria and Arlington. Springtime is also ablaze with celebrations of the season that lure us outdoors. The Cherry Blossom Festival in early April beckons visitors from around the world. Crew season draws us to the Potomac River for regattas. The last week in April marks Virginia Historic Garden Week, when communities throughout the state offer tours of houses and gardens in some of the Old Dominion's finest neighborhoods. And finally, horse racing dominates the first Saturday in May. The rest of the country may turn its eyes to the Kentucky Derby, but Northern Virginians know the real action is at the Gold Cup races in Middleburg.

What does this mean for residents of our region? House guests! Everybody wants to visit during springtime! Now is the time to update your collection of travel brochures, brush up on your quickie two-hour tour of the downtown memorials, check out the newest restaurants and shops in Old Town Alexandria, buy your season pass for Mount Vernon and take a deep breath. When they ask *"What Can I Bring?"* tell them comfortable shoes, curiosity, and a good appetite! Whether dining in or toting food along on your jaunts, start your guests' day off with a sumptuous brunch to sustain them during their treks. Use the delights of the season-fresh strawberries and the first asparagus to tempt their palates. They'll leave town declaring your hosting skills as the highlight of their visit!

Orange-Poppy Seed Bread

3	cups sifted all-purpose flour
1½	teaspoons baking powder
1	teaspoon salt
2⅓	cups sugar
1⅛	cups vegetable oil
3	large eggs
1½	cups milk
1½	tablespoons poppy seeds
1½	teaspoons vanilla extract
1½	teaspoons almond extract
1½	teaspoons butter or margarine
	Orange Glaze

- Combine first 3 ingredients in medium bowl and set aside.

- Beat sugar and oil at medium speed with an electric mixer 3 minutes; add eggs and milk, beating until blended. Add flour mixture, beating until blended. Add poppy seeds and next 3 ingredients, beating until blended.

- Pour batter into 2 greased and floured 8½ x 4½-inch loaf pans.

- Bake at 325° for 90 minutes.

- Remove loaves from oven and pour glaze over top. Cool in pans on a wire rack. Remove from pans, and serve.

Yields 2 loaves (12 servings each)

Orange Glaze

¼	cup orange juice
¾	cup powdered sugar
½	teaspoon vanilla extract
½	teaspoon almond extract
½	teaspoon butter or margarine

- Beat all ingredients at medium speed with an electric mixer until sugar is dissolved.

Banana-Chocolate Chip Nut Bread

1½	cups sugar
½	cup butter or shortening
2	large eggs, lightly beaten
2¼	cups all-purpose flour
½	teaspoon baking powder
¾	teaspoon baking soda
½	teaspoon salt
1	cup mashed banana
1	teaspoon vanilla extract
¼	cup buttermilk or ¼ cup milk plus a few drops of lemon juice
1	cup nuts, chopped
1	cup semisweet chocolate morsels

- Beat sugar and butter at medium speed with an electric mixer until creamy; add eggs, beating well.
- Combine flour and next 3 ingredients; add to butter mixture, beating well.
- Combine banana and next 4 ingredients; add to flour mixture, beating well. Pour batter into a greased 8½ x 4½-inch loaf pan.
- Bake at 350° for 1 hour.

Yields 1 loaf

Be creative when baking bread. Instead of a 4 x 8-inch loaf pan, substitute a 1½-quart round baking dish. Use a 2-quart baking dish in lieu of a 5 x 9-inch loaf pan.

Pumpkin Bread

⅓   cup vegetable oil

⅓   cup applesauce

2⅓   cups sugar

4   large eggs

1   (15-ounce) can pumpkin

½   teaspoon baking powder

2   teaspoons baking soda

1½   teaspoons salt

1   teaspoon ground
       cinnamon

½   teaspoon ground cloves

3⅓   cups all-purpose flour,
       sifted

⅔   cup water

- Beat first 3 ingredients at medium speed with an electric mixer until creamy; add eggs, 1 at a time, beating well after each addition. Stir in pumpkin. Add baking powder and next 4 ingredients, beating well. Add flour in thirds, beating well after each addition. Add water, beating well.

- Pour batter into 2 greased 4 x 8-inch loaf pans.

- Bake at 350° for 1 hour (for smaller loaves bake 45 to 50 minutes, for muffins bake 25 to 28 minutes, for miniature muffins bake 18 to 20 minutes).

Yields 2 (8 x 4-inch loaves)
or 12 muffins

*C*heck out the possibilities here: a great bread to have on hand in the freezer; prepare it ahead and ease the time crunch of holiday breakfasts; what a wonderful gift bread when prepared as small loaves and wrapped in patterned cellophane food wrap with a festive ribbon.

Dark Zucchini Bread

3 large eggs
1 cup vegetable oil
2 cups dark brown sugar
3 teaspoons vanilla extract
3 cups grated zucchini
2 tablespoons molasses
4 cups all-purpose flour
1 teaspoon baking soda
½ teaspoon baking powder
1 teaspoon salt
2 teaspoons ground
     cinnamon
1 teaspoon ground
     allspice
½ cup nuts (optional)

- Beat eggs at medium speed with an electric mixer; add oil and sugar, beating well. Add vanilla, zucchini, and molasses, beating well.

- Combine flour and next 5 ingredients in a separate bowl; stir in nuts, if desired. Gradually add dry ingredients to zucchini mixture, beating well.

- Pour batter into 2 greased and floured 4 x 8-inch loaf pans, filling three-fourths full.

- Bake at 350° for 1 hour. Cool in pans on a wire rack.

Yields 2 loaves (12 servings each)

*D*ark brown sugar? Light brown sugar? Nowadays, all brown sugar is simply white sugar combined with molasses. Light brown sugar has less molasses added and generally has a more delicate flavor than dark brown.

Cranberry Bread

2 cups all-purpose flour

1½ teaspoons baking powder

½ teaspoon salt

1 cup sugar

¼ cup shortening

1 tablespoon grated orange rind

¾ cup fresh orange juice

1 large egg, lightly beaten

½ cup chopped nuts

1 cup chopped cranberries

- Combine first 4 ingredients and cut in shortening with a pastry blender until mixture resembles cornmeal. Stir orange rind, juice, and egg into flour mixture. Fold in nuts and cranberries.
- Pour batter into a wax paper-lined 4 x 8-inch loaf pan.
- Bake at 350° for 1 hour.

Yields 1 loaf

Once again, a treat for the holiday table which can also become a gift-giving staple. Add variety to your gifts of baked goods by wrapping them in special colorful seasonal hand or tea towels. You'll be remembered long after the gift is eaten.

Vienna Breakfast Muffins

1½ cups plus 2 tablespoons all-purpose flour

2 teaspoons baking powder

¼ teaspoon salt

¾ cup sugar

¼ teaspoon ground nutmeg

½ cup milk

1 large egg, lightly beaten

⅓ cup butter or margarine, melted

1 teaspoon ground cinnamon

½ cup sugar

½ teaspoon vanilla extract

¼ cup butter or margarine, melted

• Combine first 5 ingredients in a bowl.

• Combine milk, egg, and ⅓ cup melted butter in a separate bowl; add to dry ingredients, stirring just until dry ingredients are moistened.

• Pour batter into unlined greased muffin pan cups, filling half full.

• Bake at 400° for 20 minutes.

• Combine cinnamon, ½ cup sugar, and vanilla in a small bowl.

• Remove muffins from oven and pan; dip muffin tops first in ¼ cup melted butter and then in sugar mixture, coating tops. Serve warm.

Yields 18 muffins

Try adding color and serving variety to your morning table when serving breakfast breads by lining a basket with a colorful cloth napkin or dish towel.

Delicious Blueberry Muffins

3   cups all-purpose flour
1   tablespoon baking
     powder
2   cups sugar
½   cup margarine, cut up
2   large eggs
1   cup milk
1   teaspoon vanilla extract
1¾ cups blueberries
2   tablespoons butter or
     margarine, melted

- Combine first 3 ingredients in a bowl; cut in margarine using a pastry blender until mixture is crumbly. Reserve 1 cup sugar mixture.

- Add eggs, milk, and vanilla to remaining mixture. Beat at medium speed with an electric mixer until smooth. Fold in blueberries.

- Pour batter into greased or lined muffin pan cups.

- Drizzle melted butter over reserved 1 cup sugar mixture, stirring slightly. Sprinkle over muffin batter.

- Bake at 350° for 20 to 25 minutes.

Yields 24 muffins

*W*hen adding blueberries or raisins to a batter, you can avoid having the fruit sink to the bottom of your baked product if you toss the fruit in a bit of the dry ingredient mixture before the liquids are added. Once the wet and dry mixtures are stirred into a batter, gently add the "dusted" fruit.

Apple Muffins

1	large egg, lightly beaten
½	cup milk
¼	cup vegetable oil
1½	apples, peeled and grated or diced
1½	cups all-purpose flour
2	teaspoons baking powder
½	teaspoon salt
½	cup sugar
½	teaspoon ground cinnamon
½	teaspoon ground allspice
¼	teaspoon ground nutmeg

- Preheat oven to 400°.
- Combine first 3 ingredients in a large bowl; stir in apple.
- Combine flour and next 6 ingredients; add to apple mixture, stirring until dry ingredients are moistened.
- Pour batter into muffin pan cups.
- Bake at 400° for 25 to 30 minutes. Serve hot.

Yields 12 muffins

For a low-fat version, substitute ¼ cup applesauce for vegetable oil.

*J*ust *what is allspice? Although it tastes like a mixture of cinnamon, cloves, and nutmeg, allspice-also called Jamaica pepper-is the whole or ground dried berry of the evergreen pimento tree.*

Crystal City Coffee Cake

1	cup chopped pecans
1	teaspoon ground cinnamon
4	teaspoons granulated sugar
1	cup butter or margarine
2	cups granulated sugar
2	large eggs
1	cup sour cream
½	teaspoon vanilla extract
2	cups sifted all-purpose flour
1	teaspoon baking powder
¼	teaspoon salt
	Powdered sugar

- Combine first 3 ingredients; set aside.
- Beat butter, 2 cups granulated sugar, and eggs at medium speed with an electric mixer until creamy. Fold in sour cream and vanilla. Fold in flour, baking powder, and salt.
- Spoon half of batter into a greased 9 x 11-inch pan; top with pecan mixture. Spoon remaining half of batter over pecan mixture.
- Bake at 350° for 1 hour. Let cool on a wire rack. Sprinkle with powdered sugar.

Yields 1 cake (12 servings)

Refrigerator Rolls

2	(¼-ounce) envelopes active dry yeast
1	cup lukewarm water
⅔	cup sugar
1	teaspoon salt
⅔	cup vegetable oil
1	cup boiling water
2	large eggs
6	cups all-purpose flour

- Combine yeast and 1 cup lukewarm water in a 2-cup measuring cup.

- Beat sugar, salt, and oil at medium speed with an electric mixer until creamy; add 1 cup boiling water, beating well. Add yeast mixture, beating well. Add eggs, stirring until blended. Gradually add 3 cups flour and beat 5 minutes. Beat in remaining 3 cups flour, 1 cup at a time, until dough pulls away from bowl (when dough begins to climb up the mixer, switch to a wooden spoon; you may need to add more flour on humid days to get dough to pull away from bowl).

- Chill 2 hours or up to a week, pushing dough down each day.

- Make into rolls or bread loaves. Let rise in greased pans for 2 hours in a warm oven.

- Bake rolls at 350° for 15 to 20 minutes (bread at 400° for 25 to 30 minutes).

Yields 24 rolls or 2 (8-inch) loaves

Rolls are best if chilled at least overnight.

This roll recipe may be especially appreciated at busy holiday times, for it will-with a bit of attention-remain good for one week.

Sweet Potato Rolls

2   (¼-ounce) envelopes
    active dry yeast
1½ cups warm water (105°
    to 115°)
3   cups whole wheat flour
3   cups all-purpose flour
½   cup firmly packed
    brown sugar
1¼ teaspoons salt
½   cup margarine, softened
2   large eggs
1   (16-ounce) can sliced
    sweet potatoes,
    drained

- Process yeast and 1½ cups warm water in a food processor or mixer with a dough hook 30 seconds. Let stand at room temperature 5 minutes.

- Combine flours in a large bowl. Add 1 cup flour mixture, brown sugar, and next 4 ingredients to yeast mixture; process until smooth, stopping to scrape down sides.

- Gradually stir flour mixture into remaining yeast mixture to make a soft dough. Process 5 minutes or until smooth and elastic.

- Place dough in a well-greased bowl, turning to grease top. Cover and let rise in a warm place (85°), free from drafts, 1 hour or until doubled in bulk.

- Punch dough down, and divide in half. Shape each portion into a ball. Roll each ball into a 16-inch circle on a floured surface; cut each circle into 16 wedges. Roll up wedges, beginning at wide end; place, point side down, on a greased baking sheet.

- Cover and let rise in a warm place, free from drafts, 30 minutes or until doubled in bulk.

- Bake at 350° for 15 minutes or until golden brown.

Yields 32 rolls

Dough may be made ahead. Knead, place in greased bowl, and cover securely with plastic wrap. Chill at least 6 hours. Punch down, and proceed as directed.

While found in most Latin American markets, true yams are not widely marketed in the United States, so chances are what's available at your grocery store is a sweet potato. The sweet potato is higher in vitamins A and C than the yam, which tends to be higher in both sugar and moisture content. In most recipes, one can be substituted for the other.

Salmon Quiche

1   cup whole wheat flour

⅔   cup shredded cheddar
      cheese

¼   cup finely chopped
      onion

½   teaspoon salt

¼   teaspoon pepper

6   tablespoons vegetable
      oil

1   (15½-ounce) can red
      salmon, drained with
      liquid reserved

3   large eggs, lightly beaten

1   cup sour cream

¼   cup mayonnaise

½   cup (2 ounces) shredded
      cheddar cheese

1   teaspoon dried onion

¼   teaspoon dried dill weed

- Combine first 6 ingredients;
  reserve ½ cup mixture. Press
  remaining mixture into a 9-inch
  round cake pan.

- Bake at 400° for 10 minutes.

- Add enough water to reserved
  salmon liquid to make a ½ cup.
  Beat salmon liquid, eggs, sour
  cream, and mayonnaise at medium speed with an electric mixer
  until blended. Stir in salmon, ½
  cup cheddar cheese, dried onion,
  and dill weed.

- Spoon salmon mixture into
  prepared crust. Sprinkle reserved
  ½ cup flour mixture over top.

- Bake at 325° for 45 minutes.

Serves 6

Vegetable Quiche

2   cups chopped onion

1   garlic clove, minced

2   tablespoons olive oil

3   tablespoons chopped
    fresh or 1 tablespoon
    dried basil

¼   teaspoon salt

4   large eggs, lightly beaten

1   cup milk

¼   teaspoon dry mustard

1   tablespoon all-purpose
    flour

⅓   cup grated Parmesan
    cheese

¾   cup (3 ounces) shredded
    mozzarella cheese

1   (9-inch) pastry shell

⅓   cup sliced black olives

1   medium tomato, thinly
    sliced

• Sauté onion and garlic in hot oil in
  a skillet until tender and golden;
  stir in basil and salt.

• Whisk together eggs and next
  3 ingredients.

• Combine cheeses and sprinkle
  ½ cup mixture into pastry shell.
  Spread onion mixture over cheese
  and sprinkle with olives. Pour egg
  mixture over olives and sprinkle
  with remaining cheese. Arrange
  tomato on top.

• Bake at 375° for 40 to 45 minutes
  or until set.

Serves 6 to 8

Prebaking pie crusts: Shrinkage of your pie crust is minimized if you freeze it before baking.

Garden Fresh Frittata

4	large eggs, lightly beaten
3	cups shredded zucchini
2	cups shredded carrots
1½	cups all-purpose flour
¾	cup mayonnaise
1	cup (4 ounces) shredded cheddar cheese
½	cup grated Parmesan cheese
¼	cup chopped onion
1	tablespoon chopped fresh basil
	Freshly ground black pepper to taste

- Combine all ingredients; pour into a buttered quiche pan.
- Bake at 375° for 30 to 35 minutes or until set.

Serves 6 to 8

When fresh zucchini overwhelms your own or a neighbor's garden, wash, shred, and freeze it to have on hand for this dish.
Many children can be "persuaded" to eat their veggies when they're hidden in a cheesy egg dish such as this one.

Tomato and Onion Tart

2   large sweet onions (about 1½ pounds), thinly sliced

2   tablespoons olive oil

    Salt and pepper to taste

1   (15-ounce) package refrigerated pie crusts

2   cups (8 ounces) shredded dry Jack or Monterey Jack cheese

½   pound plum tomatoes, cut into ½-inch wedges

½   pound medium-size yellow tomatoes (about 2) or ½ pound yellow plum tomatoes, cut into ½-inch wedges

¼   cup niçoise olives, pitted

- Preheat oven to 375°.

- Cook onions in olive oil salted to taste, covered, in a large heavy skillet over medium heat, stirring occasionally, 20 minutes or until soft. Uncover and cook, stirring occasionally, until onion is golden and liquid has evaporated. Remove skillet from heat.

- Unfold pie crust and fit in a 12-inch tart pan with removable bottom or quiche dish according to package directions. Trim overhang to ¾ inch, reserving remainder for another use. Fold overhang toward center and press against side of pan.

- Spread onion mixture over crust and top with cheese. Arrange tomatoes and olives in concentric circles over cheese, beginning at the outside and dividing the area into quarters alternating quarters with red and yellow tomato. Repeat with the inner circle. Season with salt and pepper to taste.

- Bake at 375° for 1 hour and 15 minutes or until pastry is golden. Let cool on a wire rack. Remove rim of pan to serve.

Serves 6 to 8 as a main dish or 12 to 16 as an appetizer

This tart makes a beautiful addition to a buffet.

Fruited Sausage Casserole

1 pound mild bulk pork
   sausage
1 (29-ounce) can peach
   halves, drained with ¼
   cup juice reserved
¼ cup firmly packed
   brown sugar
½ teaspoon ground
   cinnamon
¼ teaspoon ground cloves

- Brown sausage in a skillet over medium heat, stirring until it crumbles and is no longer pink; drain well.

- Place peach halves, cut side up, in a well-greased 6 x 10-inch baking dish.

- Combine brown sugar, cinnamon, and cloves, stirring well. Sprinkle over peach halves. Drizzle with reserved peach juice.

- Bake at 450° for 15 minutes. Remove from oven and sprinkle with sausage.

- Bake 15 more minutes.

Serves 6

Sausage and Salsa Casserole

½ tablespoon butter or margarine

1 pound bulk sausage

¼ teaspoon hot sauce

6-7 large mushrooms, sliced

6 large eggs

1 (8-ounce) container sour cream

1 teaspoon dried parsley

½ teaspoon ground cumin

½ teaspoon salt

½ teaspoon pepper

2 cups (8 ounces) shredded Monterey Jack cheese

1 (4.5-ounce) can chopped green chiles, drained

1½ cups salsa

1 cup (4 ounces) shredded cheddar cheese

- Preheat oven to 400°.
- Melt butter in an 8 x 12-inch baking dish and tilt to cover sides and bottom of dish.
- Brown sausage in a skillet over medium heat, stirring until it crumbles and is no longer pink; add hot sauce and mushrooms. Cook 2 minutes. Drain, and set aside.
- Whisk together eggs and sour cream; add parsley and next 3 ingredients. Pour egg mixture into prepared dish and bake at 400° for 10 to 12 minutes or until eggs are softly set, stirring eggs from outside to center every 4 minutes and being careful not to overcook.
- Sprinkle egg mixture with Monterey Jack cheese; top with chiles. Spoon sausage mixture over top. Spoon salsa evenly over top and sprinkle with cheddar cheese. Cover and chill until ready to bake.
- Bring to room temperature. Bake at 325° for 30 minutes. Let stand at room temperature 5 minutes before serving.

Serves 10 to 12

If you need to add color to your brunch table, garnish top liberally with sprigs of fresh parsley or cilantro.

Brunch Casserole

⅓ cup butter or margarine

¼ cup all-purpose flour

Pinch of salt

1 cup cream

1 cup milk

½ teaspoon dried basil

½ teaspoon dried thyme

1 pound shredded sharp cheddar cheese

1½ dozen hard-cooked eggs, sliced

1 pound bacon, cooked and crumbled

¼ cup chopped fresh parsley

Buttered breadcrumbs

- Melt butter in a large saucepan over medium heat; add flour and next 5 ingredients. Cook, stirring often, until creamy. Add cheese, stirring until melted.

- Place 6 sliced eggs in the bottom of a 9 x 13 x 2-inch baking dish. Layer with one-third each of bacon, parsley, and cream sauce. Repeat layers twice using remaining egg, bacon, parsley, and sauce. Top with breadcrumbs.

- Bake at 350° for 30 minutes.

Serves 10

Because this casserole freezes well, don't cook it first. Try it at your next holiday breakfast. Just be certain to remove it from the freezer the night before, and allow it to thaw in the refrigerator overnight.

Garlic-Cheese Grits

3	cups water
1	cup quick-cooking grits
1	teaspoon salt
4	tablespoons butter or margarine
1	cup milk
4	large eggs, lightly beaten
2	cups (8 ounces) shredded cheddar cheese
1	(4- to 5-ounce) roll garlic cheese

- Bring water to a boil in a saucepan; add grits and salt. Cook according to package directions.

- Bring 1 cup water to a boil in the bottom of a double boiler. Melt butter in the top of double boiler. Combine milk and eggs. Gradually add to butter, stirring constantly. Cook, stirring constantly, until thickened. Stir in cheese.

- Combine grits and cheese mixture. Pour into a greased 2-quart baking dish.

- Bake at 350° for 45 minutes.

Serves 4 to 6

*G*rits, they're not just for breakfast anymore! And they're not just for Southerners! Victims of bad press in the past, grits-generally corn these days but technically referred to as coarsely ground grain of rice, oats, or corn-are showing up on the dinner menus of fine restaurants throughout the country. In your home try them with pork chops, tenderloin, or a ham steak.

Long a Southern tradition, grits are moving into the mainstream as people acknowledge their likeness to Italian polenta and Mexican masa harina. All three are made from corn ground into meal-polenta and masa harina are generally a finer grind than grits.

Apple Noodle Pudding

½ pound flat egg noodles, cooked

4 large eggs or 1 cup egg substitute

8 ounces creamed cottage cheese

½ cup butter or margarine, melted

½ cup sugar

1 cup milk

3 apples, peeled and sliced

½ teaspoon cinnamon sugar

- Combine first 6 ingredients, tossing gently. Spoon into a greased 2-quart baking dish. Place apple slices on top and sprinkle with cinnamon sugar.
- Bake at 375° for 1 hour.

Serves 8

To make your own cinnamon sugar, combine ½ cup granulated sugar with 1 to 2 teaspoons of ground cinnamon, or to taste. Keep in a cleaned spice jar, and use for assorted recipes and a snowy morning's Cinnamon Toast.

Cinnamon-Raisin Breakfast Pudding

1	unsliced cinnamon-raisin bread loaf
5	large eggs
3	egg yolks
¾	cup milk
1	cup half-and-half
1	tablespoon vanilla extract
1	teaspoon ground cinnamon
½	teaspoon ground nutmeg
½	cup butter or margarine, melted
	Powdered sugar

- Trim crusts from bread and cut into 8 slices.

- Grease 2 (9-inch) square pans and arrange 4 slices in each pan.

- Whisk together whole eggs and next 6 ingredients; pour half of mixture into each pan. Cover pans with aluminum foil and chill overnight.

- Preheat oven to 350°.

- Drizzle casseroles evenly with melted butter. Bake 45 to 60 minutes. Sprinkle with powdered sugar and serve.

Serves 8 to 10

Your best source for unsliced cinnamon-raisin bread which is called for here, is a bakery.

A good bet for a hectic festive morning, as this pudding needs to be assembled ahead of time and chilled overnight.

Franklin Farms French Toast

1   large orange

6   large eggs, lightly beaten

¼   teaspoon ground cardamom, cinnamon, nutmeg or 1 teaspoon vanilla

½   cup butter or margarine

12   white bread slices, cut in half diagonally

- Preheat oven to 450°.

- Grate 1 tablespoon orange rind into a shallow dish. Cut orange in half and squeeze ⅓ cup juice into a measuring cup. Whisk juice, eggs, and cardamom into orange rind.

- Place butter evenly on 2 (10 x 15-inch) jelly-roll pans; place in oven until butter is melted.

- Dip bread slices in egg mixture, coating all sides. Place slices in a single layer in pans.

- Bake at 450° for 5 minutes on each side. Serve with maple syrup.

Serves 6

Need a quick breakfast idea? Leftover French toast, waffles, and pancakes can be frozen and reheated quickly on a busy workday morning. French toast and waffles reheat quickly in your pop-up toaster. Pancakes, however, reheat better in a layer in the oven, toaster oven, or microwave.

Heavenly Pancakes

1	cup all-purpose flour
½	teaspoon baking soda
1	teaspoon baking powder
1	large egg, separated
1	cup buttermilk
2	tablespoons butter or margarine, melted
2	tablespoons oil, bacon fat, or butter

- Combine first 3 ingredients.
- Lightly whisk together egg yolk, buttermilk, and butter in a large bowl.
- Beat egg white in a small bowl at medium speed with a hand-held mixer until soft peaks form.
- Add flour mixture to buttermilk mixture, beating lightly with a hand-held mixer just until dry ingredients are moistened (do not overmix). Fold in egg white.
- Cook pancakes, 4 or 5 at a time, in hot oil in a large nonstick skillet over medium-high heat until bubbles form on top, using a large spoon to scoop batter. Flip once, and cook until done.

Serves 2 to 3

If buttermilk is unavailable, you can substitute 1 cup milk plus 1½ teaspoons baking powder and 1 tablespoon butter.

It's always fun to make pancakes in interesting shapes; numbers and letters are a hit too. Designing your creations is a breeze if you save plastic squeeze bottles-jelly and mustard ones work well. Wash the bottles thoroughly, then fill with pancake batter and start creating. If the batter is too thick to squeeze, add a little milk and shake well. Always a treat, add red food coloring on Valentine's Day or green food coloring for St. Patrick's Day.

Grape Salad

1	pound red grapes
1	pound green grapes
1	(8-ounce) package cream cheese, softened
½	cup granulated sugar
1	(8-ounce) container sour cream
1	tablespoon vanilla extract
1	cup firmly packed brown sugar
¾	cup chopped pecans

- Place grapes in a large serving bowl.
- Combine cream cheese and granulated sugar, stirring well.
- Combine sour cream and vanilla in a separate bowl.
- Combine cream cheese mixture and sour cream mixture. Add to grapes, stirring well. Top with brown sugar and pecans (do not stir).
- Cover and chill overnight.

Serves 8 to 10

Strawberries Excellent

1 (3-ounce) package regular or light cream cheese

½ cup firmly packed brown sugar

1½ cups regular or light sour cream

2 tablespoons Grand Marnier liqueur

1 quart strawberries (with stems)

- Beat first 4 ingredients at medium speed with an electric mixer until smooth. Chill up to 6 hours.

- Arrange strawberries on a serving platter and serve with dip.

Serves 8

Let seasonal specialties determine the fruit you use here. Fresh melon-cantaloupe and honeydew are two of our favorites-fresh pineapple spears, red or green seedless grapes . . . or try another family favorite. All can supplement the strawberries here for a beautiful presentation.

Hospitality Casserole

1½ cups (6 ounces) shredded cheddar cheese

¾ cup sugar

6 tablespoons all-purpose flour

2 (20-ounce) cans pineapple chunks in juice, drained with juice reserved

1⅓ stacks round buttery crackers, crushed

½ cup butter or margarine, melted

• Combine first 3 ingredients; add pineapple and ½ cup reserved juice, stirring well. Spoon into a greased 9-inch square baking dish. Sprinkle with crushed crackers and drizzle with melted butter.

• Bake at 350° for 30 minutes. Serve immediately.

Serves 8

Your little ones love to help in the kitchen, but tend to create more mess than help? Let them assist with this recipe, for even toddlers can handle crushing the crackers if the zip-top bag is tightly closed and rules about not bashing a sibling with the rolling pin are well-enforced!

Generally speaking, 16 ounces of cheese in a block yields 4 to 4½ cups shredded cheese. For 6 ounces, use 1½ to 1¾ cups shredded.

Complements

Al Fresco Dining

Gold Cup Cheese Spread, *page 18*

Crunchy Chicken Chopped Salad, *page 217*

Picnic Slaw, *page 229*

Potato Salad
with Horseradish-Dill Sauce, *page 218*

Apple Muffins, *page 161*

Peanut Butter Fingers, *page 238*

The Parks Are Alive With The Sound of Music

There you are, lying on a grassy lawn on a warm summer night, music swirling about, an engorged orange moon filling the horizon above, a splendidly civilized picnic supper spilling out of a lovely wicker hamper beside you, and the one you love adoringly clinking wine glasses with you. Sound romantic? Of course, you might also have a trio of little ones swaying to the beat and blithely stepping into the potato salad. Whatever your version of reality, the good news is that it can be yours practically every night of the week all summer long in Northern Virginia. One of the glories of our area is the summer concerts that grace our parks and fill our ears and hearts with every sound imaginable. We are fortunate to be the home of the National Park Service's Wolf Trap Farm Park. Here, every night from May through September, world-class musicians hold crowds captive with their creations. From the National Symphony's annual 1812 Overture (complete with cannons) to opera, rock and roll, and jazz. Wolf Trap offers something for every taste. But for more spontaneous moments, look no further than the neighborhood parks, where free concerts of every genre abound.

Of course, fabulous food only enhances the outdoor concert experience. Gather your friends and family and organize a picnic befitting the setting. Going to hear the symphony at Wolf Trap? Then pull out the champagne flutes, silver platters and candelabra. Paper plates and a red-checked tablecloth spread on the ground are perfect for a Thursday night concert at Fort Ward Park. Feature the best of summer's produce in your culinary creations. A plate of ripe luscious sliced tomatoes is legitimate response to *"What Can I Bring?"* at this time of year. Keep it simple. That's what summer is all about!

Middleburg Medley

1 medium onion, sliced

1 red bell pepper, sliced

2 tablespoons vegetable oil

3 garlic cloves, minced

2 small to medium zucchini, sliced

2 small to medium yellow squash, sliced

1 cup frozen corn kernels

1 large tomato, peeled and chopped

2 jalapeño peppers, seeded and chopped

2-3 teaspoons chopped fresh basil

½ teaspoon dried Italian seasoning

½ teaspoon salt

½ cup grated Parmesan cheese

- Sauté onion and bell pepper in hot oil in a large skillet over medium heat, stirring often, 4 minutes. Add garlic and cook 1 to 2 minutes or until vegetables are tender. Add zucchini and yellow squash, and cook, stirring often, 7 minutes. Add corn and next 5 ingredients; reduce heat and simmer, stirring often, 7 to 10 minutes.

- Sprinkle vegetable medley with Parmesan cheese. Serve immediately with cooked pasta or as a side dish.

Serves 2 to 4

Enjoy this as a main dish, served with pasta and a green salad, or as a side dish especially good with grilled seafood.

Walnut Broccoli

3   (10-ounce) packages
    frozen broccoli spears,
    cooked and drained
½   cup butter or margarine
¼   cup all-purpose flour
2½ teaspoons chicken
    bouillon granules
2   cups milk
6   tablespoons butter or
    margarine
⅔   cup water
1   (8-ounce) package herb-
    seasoned stuffing mix
1   cup walnuts, chopped
    Paprika to taste

- Preheat oven to 400°.

- Cut broccoli spears into 1-inch
  pieces; place in a greased 9 x 13
  x 2-inch baking dish.

- Melt ½ cup butter in a large
  saucepan over medium heat; stir
  in flour and bouillon granules.
  Cook, stirring constantly, 1 to
  2 minutes. Add milk; bring to a
  boil, stirring constantly. Boil,
  stirring constantly, until slightly
  thickened. Pour sauce over
  broccoli.

- Heat 6 tablespoons butter and
  ⅔ cup water in a saucepan over
  medium heat until butter is
  melted. Remove from heat and
  stir in stuffing mix and walnuts.
  Sprinkle over broccoli. Sprinkle
  casserole with paprika.

- Bake at 400° for 25 minutes until
  thoroughly heated and golden
  brown.

Serves 10 to 12

Spectacular Platter

1	small broccoli stalk
1	cup small fresh button mushrooms
½	head cauliflower, broken into flowerets
¼	pound green beans
½	cup carrot sticks
1	cup cooked garbanzo or kidney beans, drained
½	cup Zesty Herb Dressing (recipe on page 185)
½	zucchini, thinly sliced
½	green bell pepper, seeded and sliced into rings
1	tomato, cut into wedges
1	small purple onion, thinly sliced
8	ounces part-skim mozzarella, cubed
¼	cup fresh parsley, chopped

- Separate broccoli into flowerets; peel stems and slice.

- Arrange broccoli and next 4 ingredients in a steamer basket over boiling water. Cover and steam until crisp-tender.

- Combine steamed vegetables, garbanzo beans, and dressing; chill overnight. Drain vegetables, reserving marinade.

- Arrange vegetables in the center of a serving platter. Arrange zucchini and next 4 ingredients around steamed vegetables. Drizzle reserved marinade evenly over platter. Sprinkle with parsley.

Serves about 10

(Spectacular Platter continued)

Zesty Herb Dressing

¼	cup lemon juice
¼	cup wine vinegar
⅓	cup olive oil
2	teaspoons minced onion
½	teaspoon dried basil
½	teaspoon sugar
½	teaspoon paprika
½	teaspoon dry mustard
⅛	teaspoon pepper

- Whisk together all ingredients. Chill.

𝒜s a centerpiece for a buffet, this platter provides color and texture as well as spectacular flavor.

Festive Asparagus

1   bunch fresh asparagus, with tough ends removed

½   red bell pepper, seeded and cut into thin strips

Juice of 1 lemon

¼   cup balsamic vinegar

2   tablespoons Dijon mustard

1   garlic clove, minced

Dash of Worcestershire sauce

½   cup extra-virgin olive oil

Salt and freshly ground pepper to taste

Grated rind from 1 lemon

- Arrange asparagus and bell pepper in a steamer basket over boiling water; cover and steam until crisp-tender.

- Whisk together lemon juice and next 4 ingredients; gradually whisk in oil. Season with salt and pepper to taste.

- Arrange asparagus on a serving platter; top with bell pepper strips. Drizzle dressing over top and sprinkle with lemon rind. Serve immediately.

Serves 4

With its beautiful preparation, this dish will highlight your Easter or spring table. Consider serving this with baked ham or lamb.

Asparagus with Mustard-Yogurt Sauce

1   pound fresh very thin asparagus, trimmed

½   cup nonfat plain yogurt

2   tablespoons mayonnaise

2½ tablespoons Dijon mustard

1   tablespoon minced fresh dill

1   tablespoon minced fresh chives

    Freshly ground pepper to taste

- Arrange asparagus in a steamer basket over boiling water; cover and steam 3 to 5 minutes or until crisp-tender. Plunge in cold water to stop the cooking process. Drain and chill.

- Combine yogurt and next 5 ingredients; chill.

- Serve chilled asparagus with yogurt dip.

Serves 4 to 6 as a side dish,
8 as an appetizer

To serve as a side dish, place chilled asparagus on a long platter. Drizzle sauce over asparagus. To serve as an appetizer, arrange chilled asparagus on a serving platter with sauce in a dipping container on the side.

Crystal Glazed Carrots

2 teaspoons sugar

½ teaspoon ground cinnamon

¼ cup butter or margarine

5-6 carrots, peeled, sliced, and blanched

2 tablespoons orange juice

Salt and pepper to taste

10 dried apricots, slivered

⅓ cup toasted almonds

- Combine sugar and cinnamon.
- Melt butter in a skillet over medium heat; add carrots and sugar mixture. Cook over medium heat 5 minutes or until carrots are glazed. Add orange juice, salt, and pepper to taste. Stir in apricots and almonds.
- Serve immediately.

Serves 6 to 8

Cheddar-Green Bean Casserole

4 tablespoons butter or margarine, melted and divided

2 tablespoons all-purpose flour

1 teaspoon salt

¼ teaspoon pepper

1 teaspoon sugar

½ cup finely chopped onion

1 cup sour cream

2 (12-ounce) packages French-style green beans, cooked

2 cups (8 ounces) shredded cheddar cheese

½ cup cornflake crumbs

- Cook 3 tablespoons butter and flour in a saucepan over medium-low heat. Remove from heat and stir in salt and next 4 ingredients. Fold in green beans. Spoon into a shallow 2-quart baking dish.

- Cover casserole with cheese.

- Combine cornflake crumbs and remaining butter; sprinkle over casserole.

- Bake at 350° for 30 minutes.

Serves 8

Tomato Pie

2	cups all-purpose flour
4	teaspoons baking powder
½	cup butter or margarine
¾	cup milk
4-5	tomatoes, peeled and sliced
½	teaspoon dried basil
½	teaspoon dried chives
	Chopped green onions to taste
½	cup (2 ounces) shredded cheddar cheese
½	cup mayonnaise
2	tablespoons lemon juice

- Combine first 4 ingredients, stirring to form a dough; divide into 2 portions. Roll out 1 portion of dough on a floured surface; fit into a lightly greased pie plate.

- Combine tomatoes and next 6 ingredients. Spoon into prepared crust.

- Roll out remaining portion of dough on a floured surface and place over tomato filling.

- Bake at 400° for 25 minutes.

Serves 6 to 8

What a wonderful use of summer's fresh bounty! When your own tomato and basil plants are producing at record pace or your neighbors are sharing their overabundance, prepare this tart-like treasure and taste the warmth of the season.

Eggplant-Tomato Casserole

1 large eggplant (about 1½ pounds), peeled and sliced

1½ teaspoons salt

2 large eggs, lightly beaten

2 tablespoons butter or margarine, melted

Freshly ground black pepper to taste

2-3 tablespoons chopped onion

½ teaspoon dried oregano, crushed

½ cup dry breadcrumbs

2 large tomatoes, thinly sliced

½ cup (2 ounces) shredded cheddar cheese

¼ cup grated Parmesan cheese

Paprika to taste

- Combine eggplant slices, salt, and 1 inch boiling water in a saucepan; cover and cook 10 minutes. Drain.

- Mash eggplant; add eggs and next 5 ingredients, stirring well.

- Cover bottom of a buttered 1½-quart baking dish with half of tomato slices; top with eggplant mixture. Arrange remaining tomato slices on top.

- Combine cheeses and sprinkle over tomato. Sprinkle with paprika.

- Bake at 375° for 45 minutes.

Serves 4 to 6

The eggplant's peak season, August through September, coincides nicely with that of the tomato. Add this dish to your summer table, and taste the sunshine.

Fair Lakes Mushrooms

1	pound butter or margarine
4	pounds fresh button mushrooms, stemmed
1	quart Burgundy
1	teaspoon dried dill weed
1	teaspoon ground pepper
1	teaspoon garlic powder
2	cups boiling water
2	beef bouillon cubes
2	chicken bouillon cubes

• Bring all ingredients to a boil in a large Dutch oven over medium heat. Cover, reduce heat, and simmer 5 to 6 hours. Uncover and cook 3 to 5 hours, or until liquid is reduced. Serve warm in a chafing dish.

Serves 24 as an appetizer

To avoid making mushrooms soggy-and then tough when cooked-clean by rolling across a clean, damp (frequently rinsed) sponge.

Mushrooms with a Kick

1	cup butter or margarine
1½	cups small fresh button mushrooms, stemmed
1	(5-ounce) bottle Worcestershire sauce
3	tablespoons ground pepper
½	teaspoon salt
4	drops hot sauce

- Melt butter in a saucepan over medium heat; add mushrooms, tossing to coat. Stir in Worcestershire sauce and next 3 ingredients. Cover and cook over medium-high heat, stirring often, 20 minutes or until sauce thickens (do not let mushrooms stick to pan).

- Remove mushrooms with a slotted spoon. Serve hot.

Serves 6

These beauties are a great side dish for grilled steak or pork tenderloin.

Fresh Tomato-Basil Casserole

3   fresh tomatoes,
      quartered

1½ cups tomato puree

1   (16-ounce) can whole
      tomatoes

1   onion, chopped

     Salt and pepper to taste

½   teaspoon finely chopped
      fresh basil

¼   cup firmly packed
      brown sugar

1   cup cubed French bread

2   tablespoons butter or
      margarine, cut up

¾   cup herb-seasoned
      stuffing mix

- Combine first 8 ingredients and spoon into a greased 1½-quart baking dish.

- Cut butter into stuffing mix using a fork; sprinkle over casserole.

- Bake at 350° for 20 minutes or until bubbly.

Serves 6 to 8

Serve this summer dish—best when fresh tomatoes and basil are available—with grilled meat.

Zesty Stuffed Zucchini

1	large onion, peeled and chopped
2	tablespoons olive oil
4	medium zucchini
2	garlic cloves, minced
4	medium carrots, peeled and diced
1	teaspoon grated fresh ginger
¾	cup slivered almonds
	Salt and freshly ground pepper to taste

- Preheat oven to 375°.
- Sauté onion in hot oil in a medium saucepan 5 minutes.
- Halve zucchini lengthwise and scoop out centers leaving a shell. Chop scooped out zucchini; add chopped zucchini, garlic, carrots, and ginger to onion. Cover and cook over medium heat 10 minutes or until vegetables are tender. Remove from heat; stir in almonds and salt and pepper to taste.
- Place zucchini shells in a greased 9 x 13 x 2-inch baking dish. Fill shells evenly with onion mixture and cover with aluminum foil.
- Bake at 375° for 40 minutes or until shells are tender when pierced with a fork. Serve immediately.

Serves 4

*S*erve this for a special occasion, and see your guests enjoy this low-fat, flavorful treat.

Southern Corn Pudding

½   cup butter or margarine

½   cup all-purpose flour

2   teaspoons salt

4½ heaping teaspoons sugar

3½ cups milk

6   cups frozen corn kernels

6   large eggs, beaten until frothy

- Preheat oven to 350°.

- Melt butter in a large saucepan over medium heat; stir in flour, salt, and sugar. Cook, stirring constantly, until a thick paste forms. Gradually add milk, stirring until liquid is thickened. Stir in corn and eggs. Cook 5 minutes. Pour into a buttered 2½ quart baking dish.

- Bake in a water bath at 350° for 1½ hours.

Serves 12

The appearance of corn pudding on the Southern Thanksgiving table is a tribute to the first Thanksgiving, generally acknowledged to be a Virginia event. The earliest Europeans who came to the New World had never seen corn before, but grew quickly to appreciate its versatility and usefulness. See water bath notes at Lemon Fluff Pudding, page 244, under Desserts.

Pumpkin Puff

1 (29-ounce) can solid-
   pack pumpkin
⅓ cup firmly packed
   brown sugar
5 tablespoons butter or
   margarine, melted
1 teaspoon salt
½ teaspoon ground
   nutmeg
½ teaspoon ground
   cinnamon
½ teaspoon ground ginger
3 large eggs, well beaten
½ cup cream or half-and-
   half
2 tablespoons honey
½ cup chopped walnuts

- Combine first 7 ingredients; add
  eggs and cream, stirring well.
  Spoon mixture into a 2½ quart
  greased baking dish. Drizzle with
  honey and sprinkle with walnuts.
- Bake at 375° for 50 minutes or
  until slightly puffed. Serve immediately.

Serves 4 to 6

Holiday Sweet Potatoes

3	pounds sweet potatoes, peeled and cubed
¾	cup firmly packed brown sugar
3	tablespoons butter or margarine
½	teaspoon ground nutmeg
¼	teaspoon salt
1	cup milk
½	teaspoon ground cinnamon

- Boil sweet potatoes in water to cover in a saucepan until tender; let cool slightly. Process potatoes in a food processor until smooth. Add brown sugar and next 5 ingredients. Process until smooth. Spoon mixture into a greased 9 x 13 x 2-inch baking dish.

- Bake at 400° for 30 minutes.

Serves 8 to 10

*V*egetables retain more of their nutrients-and you get the benefit of these nutrients-when cooked in a minimum amount of water.

Sweet Potato Casserole

3-4 medium sweet potatoes
1 cup sugar
¼ cup butter or margarine
2 large eggs
½ teaspoon vanilla extract
¼ cup butter or margarine, melted
½ cup all-purpose flour
1 cup firmly packed brown sugar
1 cup chopped nuts

- Boil sweet potatoes in water to cover in a saucepan until tender; let cool slightly. Peel potatoes and process pulp in a food processor until smooth.

- Add sugar and next 3 ingredients. Process until smooth. Spoon mixture into a 9 x 13 x 2-inch baking dish.

- Bake at 400° for 20 to 25 minutes or until slightly puffed. Remove from oven.

- Combine melted butter and next 3 ingredients; spread over potato mixture.

- Bake 10 more minutes or until lightly browned.

Serves 8 to 10

This favorite, at many Virginia holiday meals, accompanies ham, turkey, roast chicken, and other "holiday" menus. The potato mixture can be made ahead and frozen, helping to ease the "big day" frenzy of preparations. Be sure to thaw overnight in the refrigerator, then add the topping and bake in your already-busy holiday oven.

Garlic Mashed Potatoes

2 pounds red new potatoes

6 garlic cloves

3-4 tablespoons garlic oil

4-6 ounces light or nonfat sour cream, at room temperature

½ cup warmed milk

¼ cup grated Parmesan cheese

Salt and freshly ground pepper to taste

- Halve or quarter potatoes depending on size.

- Boil potato and garlic in salted water to cover in a large saucepan 20 minutes; drain. Mash half of mixture in a bowl until lumpy.

- Add oil and half of sour cream to mashed potato mixture; gradually add warm milk continuing to mash. Stir in remaining half of potato mixture, cheese, and remaining sour cream.

- Season with salt and pepper to taste. Serve immediately.

Serves 4 to 6

Try this rustic favorite with grilled meats, especially flank steak.

Herbed Baby Red Potatoes

2   pounds red new
     potatoes
3-4 tablespoons olive oil
1   garlic clove, minced
1   teaspoon salt
1   tablespoon chopped
     fresh rosemary
1   tablespoon chopped
     fresh or 1 teaspoon
     dried thyme

- Combine potatoes and hot oil in a saucepan, stirring to coat; cook over medium heat, stirring occasionally, 25 to 35 minutes or until browned. Add garlic and next 3 ingredients, tossing well. Cover and cook until potatoes are tender and well browned.

Serves 4 to 6

These potatoes are great served with grilled meats, chicken, or fish.

Great Falls Potatoes

8-10 medium potatoes,
    peeled

1   (8-ounce) package cream
    cheese, softened

1   (8-ounce) container sour
    cream

½   cup butter or margarine,
    melted

¼   cup chopped chives

⅛   teaspoon garlic powder

2   teaspoons salt

    Paprika to taste

- Cook potatoes in boiling water to cover in a saucepan 30 minutes or until tender; drain and mash.

- Beat cream cheese at medium speed with an electric mixer until smooth; add potatoes, sour cream, and next 4 ingredients. Beat just until blended.

- Spoon mixture into a lightly buttered, 2-quart baking dish. Sprinkle with paprika. Cover and chill overnight.

- Remove from refrigerator and let stand at room temperature 15 minutes.

- Bake, uncovered, at 350° for 30 minutes, or until bubbly.

Serves 6 to 8

Save your potato water, which can be stored in the refrigerator 3 to 4 days, to use in soups and sauces (adds nutrition and flavor as well as body from the potato starch) or as a "secret ingredient" in your next chocolate cake (substituting for whatever liquid is called for).

Cheesy Scalloped Potatoes

3   tablespoons butter or margarine

2   tablespoons all-purpose flour

2   teaspoons salt
    Pepper to taste

2   cups hot milk

1½ cups (6 ounces) shredded cheddar cheese

6   potatoes, peeled and sliced

1   small onion, chopped

- Melt butter in a double boiler or saucepan over medium heat; add flour, salt, and pepper. Cook, stirring constantly, until smooth. Gradually stir in hot milk; cook, stirring constantly, until thickened. Add cheese and cook, stirring constantly, until melted.

- Layer one-third each of potato slices, onion, and cheese sauce in a lightly greased 9 x 13 x 2-inch baking dish. Repeat layers twice.

- Bake at 350° for 1 hour.

Serves 6

Another use for potato water is in your favorite recipe for bread; substitute in equal amounts for the liquid called for in the recipe.

Oven-Roasted Vegetables

2   baby eggplants, sliced into 1-inch pieces

12-16 red new potatoes

2   red bell peppers, seeded and cut into 1-inch squares

2   zucchini, peeled and cut into 1-inch slices

½   pound green beans, broken into 3 pieces each

1   large purple onion, cut into 1-inch wedges

2   cups baby carrots

1   lemon, sliced

2   tablespoons olive oil

     Salt and pepper to taste

2   fresh rosemary sprigs

- Preheat oven to 375°.

- Combine first 8 ingredients in a large roasting pan; drizzle with oil and season with salt and pepper. Place rosemary sprigs on top of mixture.

- Bake at 375°, toss every 15 to 20 minutes, 1½ hours, or until vegetables are tender.

Serves 8

Roasted Eggplant Risotto

4	garlic cloves, unpeeled
1	medium eggplant, sliced
¼	cup olive oil
2	cups chicken broth
½	cup white wine
½	cup water
1	shallot, chopped
1	tablespoon olive oil
2	tomatoes, cut into chunks
1	cup Arborio rice
½	cup fresh basil, chopped
½	cup grated Parmesan cheese
1	cup fat-free ricotta cheese

- Wrap garlic in aluminum foil and bake at 400° for 30 minutes or until tender. Let cool; peel and chop.

- Brush eggplant slices with ¼ cup oil; bake at 400° for 20 minutes on each side. Let cool; chop slices.

- Bring broth, wine, and ½ cup water to a boil in a saucepan; reduce heat and simmer.

- Sauté shallot in 1 tablespoon hot oil in a separate saucepan until tender; add tomatoes and cook until it breaks down. Add rice and cook 2 minutes or until glistening. Add ½ cup broth mixture and cook, stirring occasionally, until liquid is almost absorbed. Repeat procedure with remaining broth mixture.

- Combine chopped garlic, basil, and cheeses; add to risotto. Stir in chopped eggplant and serve immediately.

Serves 4

Because the eggplant is brushed with olive oil and roasted, this dish has much less fat than fried eggplant. Try this roasting technique for your other recipes that call for fried eggplant.

Portobello Mushroom Risotto with Feta Cheese

2 cups chopped sweet onion

2 garlic cloves, minced

2 teaspoons olive oil

1½ cups uncooked Arborio rice

2 (14½-ounce) cans chicken broth

¼ teaspoon garlic salt

¼ cup chopped fresh or 1 tablespoon dried basil

Freshly ground pepper to taste

Grilled Portobello Mushroom Slices

½ cup crumbled feta cheese

- Sauté onion and garlic in hot oil in a saucepan 1 minute; stir in rice. Add ½ cup chicken broth and cook, stirring constantly, until liquid is nearly absorbed. Repeat procedure with remaining chicken broth.

- Add garlic salt, basil, and pepper to rice mixture. Stir in Grilled Portobello Mushroom Slices. Remove from heat and stir in feta cheese. Serve immediately.

(Portobello Mushroom Risotto with Feta Cheese continued)

Grilled Portobello Mushroom Slices

1   portobello mushroom,
    stemmed

2   teaspoons olive oil

1   tablespoon balsamic
    vinegar

1   teaspoon dried basil

- Brush dirt off mushroom but do not rinse.

- Combine oil, vinegar, and basil. Brush mixture on top and bottom of mushroom; place mushroom on a rack in a broiler pan.

- Bake at 500° for 2½ to 3½ minutes on each side. Let cool; cut into slices.

Serves 6

*P*ortobello mushrooms are new to some Virginia kitchens and supermarkets. This unique dish is a great addition to your repertoire, and a way to spread your reputation as a gourmet. Use the freshest, high-quality ingredients, especially the feta cheese, for best performance.

Potomac Falls Polenta

7-8 cups skim, low-fat, or
     whole milk or
     buttermilk

2   cups yellow grits

1   cup (4 ounces) shredded
     mozzarella or Asiago
     cheese

1   cup tomato sauce

½ cup sun-dried tomatoes
     packed in oil

- Heat milk in a saucepan over medium-low heat; gradually stir in grits. Reduce heat and cook until grits are soft. Spoon half of grits into a greased 9 x 13 x 2-inch baking dish. Top with half of each of the remaining ingredients: cheese, tomato sauce, and dried tomatoes. Repeat layers once.

- Bake at 350° for 20 to 30 minutes or until cheese melts.

Serves 10

A continental twist on a Southern specialty-grits!

Seasoned Basmati Rice

2 cups basmati rice
2 cups cool water
2 tablespoons butter or margarine
1 small onion, chopped
1 teaspoon ground cardamom
1 teaspoon saffron threads (optional)
3 cups water
   Salt to taste

- Rinse rice 3 times in cool water to remove starch. Soak rice in 2 cups cool water for 30 minutes.

- Melt butter in a medium saucepan over medium heat; add onion, cardamom, and, if desired, saffron threads, and sauté 5 minutes.

- Drain rice, and add to onion mixture, stirring to coat. Add 2 cups water; cover and bring to a boil. Reduce heat and add remaining 1 cup water. Cover and simmer 20 minutes or until liquid is absorbed and rice is tender. Add salt to taste.

Serves 6 to 8

Although basmati rice is found in many local supermarkets, some may want to check out Indian and Middle Eastern markets for the real thing.

Vidalia Onion and Rice Casserole

½ cup butter or margarine

2½ pounds Vidalia onions, peeled and thinly sliced

1 cup uncooked rice

2 cups water

1½ cups (6 ounces) shredded Swiss cheese

1⅓ cups half-and-half

• Preheat oven to 325°.

• Melt butter in a skillet over medium heat; add onion slices and sauté 12 minutes or until tender.

• Bring rice and 2 cups water to a boil in a saucepan; cover and boil 15 minutes. Drain well.

• Combine onion, rice, cheese, and half-and-half and pour into a greased 9 x 13 x 2-inch baking dish. Bake at 325° for 1 hour.

Serves 8

The flavor of the casserole is enhanced when baked a day ahead. Cover and chill overnight; to reheat bake at 325° for 20 minutes.

It's worth trying to find genuine Vidalia onions for this dish. Once available only about six weeks from mid-May to the first of July, newer storage and transportation methods have increased the availability of this onion, which is as sweet as an apple and eaten like an apple by many near its Georgia "home." By Georgia state law, the name "Vidalia" can only be given to an onion grown within about 35 miles of the city of Vidalia, Georgia.

Baked Rice Pilaf

2-3	tablespoons butter or margarine
1	medium onion, finely chopped
½	cup finely chopped celery
6	medium mushrooms, thinly sliced
1½	cups uncooked rice
¼	teaspoon dried sage
1	tablespoon fresh parsley, minced
½	teaspoon salt
¼	teaspoon dried basil
3½	cups chicken broth

- Melt butter in a saucepan over medium heat; add onion, celery, and mushrooms, and sauté until tender (do not brown). Add rice and sauté 1 to 2 minutes (do not brown). Stir in sage and next 3 ingredients; spoon mixture into a greased 2-quart baking dish.

- Bring broth to a boil; stir into casserole.

- Bake, covered, at 350° for 35 minutes.

Serves 6 to 8

Confetti Rice

1   large can Italian tomatoes, drained and chopped

2   (4.5-ounce) cans chopped green chiles, drained

1   medium jar pimiento-stuffed olives, drained and sliced

1   large onion, chopped

4   cups (1 pound) shredded longhorn cheese

1   cup uncooked converted rice

½   cup olive oil

1   cup boiling water

- Combine all ingredients and pour into a greased 9 x 13 x 2-inch baking dish.

- Bake, covered, at 250° for 2 to 3 hours.

Serves 6 to 8

This is a perfect dish for a casual dinner party. All the ingredients (except the oil and boiling water) can be combined up to a day in advance. Just stir in the oil and boiling water right before baking. In addition, the 2 to 3 hours baking time will allow you to spend time with your guests, rather than in the kitchen.

Named after the cow, longhorn cheese is a mild form of cheddar.

Carrot Ambrosia Salad

3   cups shredded carrots

1   cup thin orange slices or
     1 can mandarin
     oranges, drained

¼   cup slivered dates or
     raisins

1   cup flaked coconut

½   cup sour cream

1-2 tablespoons honey

     Dash of salt

     Dash of ground ginger

- Combine first 4 ingredients in a large bowl.

- Combine sour cream and next 3 ingredients in a separate bowl; pour over carrot mixture, tossing gently to mix. Chill. Serve on lettuce-lined plates.

Serves about 6

This lovely "ladies luncheon" salad is a fine accompaniment to other salads, such as chicken or pasta salads.

Papaya Salad

½ cup sugar

½ cup vinegar

½ cup vegetable oil

2 teaspoons salt

½ teaspoon dry mustard

½ cup chopped onion

2 tablespoons papaya
  seeds

2 papayas

2 large avocados

2 heads romaine and Bibb
  lettuce, torn

- Process first 6 ingredients in a blender until smooth; add seeds and process until seeds resemble coarsely ground pepper.
- Slice papayas and avocados. Toss with lettuce or arrange on top. Serve with dressing.

Serves 8 to 10

A ripe papaya has a vivid, golden yellow skin and yields slightly to palm pressure. Keep slightly green papayas at room temperature in a paper bag, and they'll ripen quickly.

Mandarin Blue Spinach Salad

2 tablespoons butter or margarine

¾ cup pecans

1 package fresh spinach, cleaned and patted dry

1 package blue cheese (Saga preferred)

1 (6-ounce) can mandarin oranges, drain and reserve juice

¼ cup olive oil

Juice and grated rind of 1 orange (rind optional)

Salt and pepper to taste

• Melt butter in a small saucepan over medium heat; add pecans and cook until browned. Remove from heat and let cool.

• Combine spinach, cheese, and mandarin oranges in a bowl.

• Combine reserved mandarin orange juice, oil, and regular orange juice, stirring well. Season with salt and pepper to taste.

• Add pecans to salad and toss with dressing. Sprinkle with orange rind, if desired.

Serves 6

*M*ost of the canned mandarin oranges available in the United States are the small Japanese satsuma oranges, one of four varieties of this orange characterized by easy-to-slip-off skin.

Tarragon Chicken Salad

Fresh bay leaves, parsley, and thyme (enough to cover bottom of roasting pan)

2 onions, thinly sliced

8 bone-in chicken breast halves

Juice of 2 lemons

Salt and pepper to taste

4-5 tablespoons chopped fresh or 4 to 5 teaspoons dried tarragon

¾ cup sour cream

¾ cup mayonnaise

4 cups finely chopped celery

3 cups pecans, chopped

- Combine herbs and onion in a generously buttered roasting pan; top with chicken breast halves, skin side up in a single layer. Sprinkle with lemon juice and salt and pepper to taste.

- Bake at 375° for 30 to 40 minutes or until done. Do not overcook. Let cool. Remove skin and bones from chicken; chop or shred meat.

- Combine chicken, salt, pepper, and tarragon in a bowl.

- Combine sour cream and mayonnaise. Add to chicken mixture, stirring until creamy but not wet. Season to taste. Stir in celery and pecans.

Serves 8

This serves a crowd and travels well when kept cold.

Crunchy Chicken Chopped Salad

¾ cup plus 2 tablespoons
seasoned rice vinegar

3 tablespoons Dijon mustard

¾ cup plus 2 tablespoons
vegetable oil

½ cup plus 1 tablespoon
sesame oil

4 tablespoons soy sauce

5 green onions, chopped

1½ teaspoons dried, crushed
red pepper

1 pound Napa cabbage,
sliced

½ pound bok choy, sliced

1 cucumber, sliced
diagonally

6 large carrots, sliced
diagonally

1 large red bell pepper,
seeded and cut into
strips

1 cup fresh mint, chopped

6 skinned and boned chicken
breast halves

Salt and pepper to taste

1 cup lightly salted, dry
roasted peanuts, coarsely
chopped

- Whisk together vinegar and mustard in a medium bowl; gradually whisk in oils. Whisk in soy sauce. Add green onions and crushed red pepper, stirring well. Divide this marinade into three equal portions.
- Combine cabbage and next 5 ingredients in a large bowl; cover and chill up to 4 hours, if desired.
- Place chicken in a shallow dish; pour first reserved portion of marinade over top and turn chicken to coat. Cover and chill 1 hour.
- Drain chicken, discarding used marinade. Grill chicken over medium heat (350° to 375°) 4 to 5 minutes on each side, basting with second portion of reserved marinade and discarding unused portion. Remove chicken from heat and slice diagonally.
- Pour enough remaining third portion of marinade over cabbage mixture to coat, tossing gently. Season with salt and pepper to taste, if desired.
- Serve cabbage mixture on individual plates and top evenly with chicken. Drizzle with remaining marinade. Sprinkle with peanuts and serve immediately.

Serves 6

When served with crusty hot bread and a light white wine, this makes a great summer dinner that is very portable.

Potato Salad with Horseradish-Dill Sauce

2	pounds red new potatoes
½	cup finely chopped purple onion
2	large carrots, shredded
4	tablespoons mayonnaise
4	tablespoons nonfat plain yogurt
2	teaspoons Dijon mustard
2	teaspoons balsamic vinegar
2	teaspoons horseradish
4	tablespoons chopped fresh dill
	Salt and pepper to taste

- Bring potatoes to a boil in 1 inch of water in a medium saucepan; boil 15 to 20 minutes or until tender. Let cool; peel and cube. Combine potatoes, onion, and carrots in a large bowl.

- Whisk together mayonnaise and next 6 ingredients; pour over potato mixture. Chill 4 to 8 hours.

Serves 4

The flavor of Dijon mustard can range from mild to hot, so work with one you know.

Blue Cheese-Potato Salad

1   pound red new
     potatoes, cut into
     small wedges

3   tablespoons red wine
     vinegar

¼   cup olive oil

¼   teaspoon ground black
     pepper

½   teaspoon salt

¼   cup crumbled blue
     cheese, divided

1   red bell pepper, seeded
     and chopped

¼   purple onion, diced

6   bacon slices, cooked and
     crumbled

2   tablespoons minced
     fresh parsley

- Boil potatoes in salted water to cover 10 to 12 minutes or until tender. Drain and place in a large bowl.

- Whisk together vinegar and next 3 ingredients; pour over potatoes and toss to coat. Add 3 tablespoons cheese, tossing well. Add red pepper and onion, tossing well. Cover tightly and refrigerate until thoroughly chilled.

- Toss potato salad with remaining cheese, bacon, and parsley just before serving.

Serves 4 to 6

A great make-a-day-ahead dish, this portable salad offers a tasty, safe carry-along alternative to a mayonnaise-based salad. The ingredients promise a colorful accompaniment to your picnic staples.

Cascades Potato Salad

1½ pounds new potatoes, cut into bite-size pieces

½ cup crumbled feta cheese

1 bunch green onions, white and light green parts thinly sliced

½ cup freshly grated Parmesan or Romano cheese

¼ cup extra-virgin olive oil

½ cup brine-cured ripe olives, pitted and sliced

1 tablespoon red wine vinegar

⅛ teaspoon celery salt

¼ teaspoon dried thyme

Freshly ground pepper to taste

- Boil potatoes in lightly salted water in a saucepan 30 minutes or until tender. Drain and let cool.

- Combine feta and next 8 ingredients in a large bowl; add potatoes, tossing to coat. Serve warm or at room temperature.

Serves 4 to 6

A key to this salad is the use of the freshest and highest quality ingredients available.

Reston Veggie Salad

1	cup sugar
½	cup vegetable oil
¾	cup white vinegar
1	(17-ounce) can peas
1	(16-ounce) can French-style green beans
1	(16-ounce) can shoepeg corn
1	small jar pimientos, chopped
1	cup chopped celery
1	cup finely chopped carrots
1	cup seeded and chopped green bell pepper
1	cup chopped onion

- Boil first 3 ingredients in a small saucepan until sugar dissolves.
- Drain canned vegetables.
- Combine peas and next 7 ingredients in a large bowl; pour dressing over salad and chill overnight. Stir before serving.

Serves 8 to 10

Reston, a successful planned community in western Fairfax County, overshadows the historical nature of the land on which it stands. Dr. Carl Wiehle bought more than 3,000 acres of the old Thornton property in 1886 for purposes of creating a symmetrically and aesthetically pleasing planned community. He did not live to realize his dream, but we do have Wiehle Road and another planned community on his land!

Pine Nut and Olive Rice Salad

3 cups chicken broth

2 cups uncooked long-
    grain rice

¼ cup olive oil

1 cup kalamata olives,
    pitted and sliced

2 tablespoons fresh lemon
    juice

1 small head radicchio,
    chopped

4 green onions, chopped

½ cup pine nuts, lightly
    toasted

⅓ cup freshly grated
    Romano or Parmesan
    cheese

    Freshly ground pepper
    to taste

- Bring broth to a boil in a heavy
  saucepan; add rice and bring to
  a boil. Cover, reduce heat, and
  simmer 20 minutes or until liquid
  is absorbed. Let cool 5 minutes.

- Drain and fluff rice, then transfer
  to a large bowl. Add oil, tossing
  well. Add olives and next 5
  ingredients, tossing well. Season
  with pepper to taste. Serve at
  room temperature.

Serves 8 to 10

High in fat, pine nuts must be stored properly to avoid becoming rancid. Purchase in small quantities, and refrigerate up to three months or freeze up to nine months.

Lentil Salad

½	teaspoon ground turmeric
½	teaspoon ground coriander
¼	teaspoon ground red pepper
¼	teaspoon ground cloves
¼	teaspoon ground nutmeg
¼	teaspoon ground cinnamon
½	teaspoon ground mace
1	teaspoon dry mustard
1	teaspoon ground cumin
1	teaspoon salt
1	teaspoon pepper
½	cup red wine vinegar
2	tablespoons sugar
½	cup canola or corn oil
1	pound dried lentils
1	cup currants
½	cup capers
1¼	cups chopped purple onion

- Whisk together first 14 ingredients.
- Boil lentils in water to cover 5 to 6 minutes or until tender. Rinse and drain well. Combine lentils and dressing in a large bowl; marinate overnight.
- Add currants, capers, and onion to salad; marinate at least 2 hours.

Serves 8 to 10

*C*apers, the sun-dried and pickled flower bud of a bush native to the Mediterranean and parts of Asia, should be rinsed before using to remove excess salt from the brine in which they are generally packed.

Garbanzo, Feta, and Olive Salad

1   (15-ounce) can garbanzo
     beans, drained

½   cup crumbled feta
     cheese

⅓   cup sliced ripe olives

1   large tomato, seeded
     and diced

2   green onions, sliced

2   tablespoons finely
     chopped fresh parsley

4   tablespoons olive oil

2   tablespoons red wine
     vinegar

     Salt and freshly ground
     pepper to taste

½-1 teaspoon chopped fresh
     oregano (optional)

½-1 teaspoon chopped fresh
     rosemary (optional)

- Combine first 6 ingredients in a
  large bowl.

- Whisk together oil and vinegar.
  Pour over salad, tossing well.
  Season to taste with salt and
  pepper. Stir in oregano and
  rosemary, if desired.

Serves 4 to 6

Another summer wonder, this salad is especially good with grilled fish.

Summer Veggie Pasta Salad

6	ounces rotini, cooked
1	cup broccoli flowerets
1	small zucchini, thinly sliced or quartered
1	cup (4 ounces) shredded or diced cheddar cheese
½	cup shredded carrots
1	cup seeded and chopped red bell pepper
¼	teaspoon seasoned salt
¼	teaspoon pepper
⅓	cup vegetable oil
¼	cup white wine vinegar
1	tablespoon Dijon mustard
¼	cup finely chopped green onions
1	tablespoon minced fresh or 1 teaspoon dried parsley
2	garlic cloves, crushed
½	teaspoon sugar
½	teaspoon dried basil
¼	teaspoon salt
¼	teaspoon dried oregano
¼	teaspoon sweet red pepper flakes, crushed

- Combine first 8 ingredients in a large bowl.

- Combine oil and next 10 ingredients in a jar; cover tightly and shake vigorously. Pour dressing over pasta mixture, tossing well. Chill 2 to 3 hours.

Serves 8 to 10

Color, texture, and wonderful flavors–this salad promises to be a hit and improves with two to three hours of "blending time." Don't be intimidated by the length of the ingredients list. Many of these are already prepared in your grocery salad bar section.

Bean Sprout Salad

½   cup vegetable oil

¼   cup cider or red wine vinegar

¼   cup soy sauce

1   teaspoon salt

1   teaspoon freshly ground pepper

¼   cup sesame seeds

2   garlic cloves, minced

½   cup scallions, finely chopped

½   cup chopped pimiento

4   cups bean sprouts

• Combine first 9 ingredients; pour over bean sprouts, tossing to coat. Chill 1 hour.

Serves 4 to 6

To make dressing ahead, combine first 7 ingredients, and chill up to 1 day. Add pimientos before tossing with bean sprouts.

Use this to accompany an Oriental meal. Avoid adding the pimiento until you are ready to toss it with the sprouts, for the pimiento will discolor the dressing.

Tantalizing Pea Salad

1   small can smoked
      almonds

1   (14- to 16-ounce)
      package frozen petit
      pois (peas)

1   tablespoon dried chives

½-1   cup mayonnaise

1-2   teaspoons curry powder

1   (6-ounce) can water
      chestnuts, drained and
      finely chopped

- Process almonds in a food processor until coarsely ground.

- Combine all ingredients in a large
  bowl, adding more mayonnaise as
  needed to hold together but not
  saturate (keep it slightly dry).
  Cover tightly and chill overnight.

- Add more mayonnaise and curry
  powder to salad as desired before
  serving. Serve on lettuce cups.

Serves 4

*Keep ingredients for this sure-to-please special in your cupboard and
freezer, ready to mix the day before for short-notice get-togethers.*

Tomato and Basil Salad

4-5 garlic cloves, crushed

2 teaspoons salt

¼ cup red wine vinegar

2 pounds firm tomatoes, peeled and sliced

6-8 fresh basil leaves, each torn into 2 or 3 pieces

Extra-virgin olive oil

Crusty bread

- Combine first 3 ingredients; let stand at least 20 minutes.

- Arrange tomato on a serving platter and top with basil. Pour oil to coat over top. Pour marinade over top. Let stand, basting occasionally, several hours. Serve with bread.

Serves 4 to 6

Cranberry-Horseradish Relish

1 (12-ounce) bag fresh or frozen cranberries

1 small onion, quartered

½ cup sugar

¼ teaspoon salt

½ cup light sour cream

3 tablespoons prepared horseradish, drained

- Process first 4 ingredients in a food processor until coarsely chopped; stir in sour cream and horseradish. Refrigerate 1 hour or until thoroughly chilled.

Yield 2½ cups

Festive-looking and perfect for the holidays, this relish is wonderful with turkey, tenderloin, and prime rib.

Picnic Slaw

1	medium head green cabbage
1	small onion
1	green bell pepper, cored and seeded
1	(10- to 11-ounce) jar pimiento-stuffed olives, drained and chopped
1	cup sugar
1	teaspoon dry mustard
½	cup vegetable or salad oil
1	teaspoon celery seeds
½	teaspoon pepper
1	cup white vinegar

- Shred first 3 ingredients in a food processor; transfer to a large bowl. Add olives to mixture and sprinkle with sugar.
- Bring mustard and next 4 ingredients to a boil in a small saucepan for 3 minutes. Pour dressing over cabbage mixture, tossing to coat. Cover and chill at least 12 hours and up to several days.

Serves 8 to 10

Because this slaw keeps well and improves with at least 12 hours blending time, you can make it several days ahead of your big event. Mixing goes much faster with a food processor, so borrow one if you must.

Endive with Hot Bacon Dressing

3   bacon slices, cut into
       ½-inch pieces
1   large egg, lightly beaten
2   tablespoons sugar
2   tablespoons vinegar
1   head endive, snapped
       into bite-size pieces

• Cook bacon in a saucepan over medium-low heat until browned. Drain bacon, pressing between layers of paper towels.

• Combine egg, sugar, and vinegar in a 1 cup liquid measuring cup; add water to equal 1 cup. Add egg mixture to pan and cook over medium heat, stirring constantly, 4 to 5 minutes or until slightly thickened. Stir in bacon. Pour dressing over endive and serve immediately.

Serves 4

If you keep a clean pair of scissors or shears just for use in the kitchen, you can cut the slices of bacon into ½-inch pieces directly into the frying pan. These shears are great for cutting herbs, raisins, and hot pizza into bite-sizes for toddlers. Just be sure to wash them on the top rack of your dishwasher after each use.

Summer Tomato Dressing

1	large vine-ripened summer tomato, peeled and pureed
⅓	cup cider vinegar
½	cup sugar
1	teaspoon dry mustard
1	teaspoon salt
¼	small onion, finely chopped
1	tablespoon celery seeds
1	cup vegetable oil

• Combine tomato and vinegar in a bowl; add sugar and next 4 ingredients, stirring after each addition. Gradually whisk in oil.

Yields 1½ to 2 cups

*T*omatoes-sweet and warm from the plants in your own backyard-are truly the treat of the Southern summer garden. Through the centuries, the folklore surrounding the tomato, which is native to South America, has led from believing they were poisonous to considering them an aphrodisiac.

Curry-Almond Dressing

3 cups mayonnaise

¾ teaspoon ground ginger

5 teaspoons curry powder

3 garlic cloves, crushed

½ cup honey

½ cup lime juice

 Dash of ground white pepper

 Salad greens

¼ cup slivered almonds

- Process first 7 ingredients in a blender until smooth. Toss dressing with salad greens and almonds.

Yields 4 cups

*C*urry powder varies widely in strength, so if your taste buds are sensitive, start with a small amount and add to taste up to recipe's instructions.

Desserts

Dessert Delights

Sterling Sugar Cookies, page 235

Layered Lemon Cheesecake, page 259

Tiramisu, page 245

Black Russian Cake, page 263

Blueberry Upside-Down Cake, page 257

Nutty Fudge Pie, page 253

Party Pecans, page 41

Coffee Bar
(including Holiday Irish Coffee Eggnog), page 43

The Evening is Young

Into every life some glamour must fall. When it's your turn, put on your party clothes and do the town. The choices for your evening's entertainment are endless. Perhaps the theatre or serious music calls you. You can always head into D.C. to the Kennedy Center, but there is a lot going on right here in Northern Virginia, too. The George Mason Center for the Performing Arts is a wonderful recent addition to our community, offering internationally acclaimed musicians and theatre. No fewer than seven regional symphony orchestras also present lovely opportunities for a night out. And let's not overlook charity balls and fundraisers. We all have a few favorites that we support and love, in part because they give us an excuse to step out in style. Art gallery and museum exhibition openings offer another venue. Whatever your pleasure, take advantage of the ample opportunities.

Your fun doesn't have to end with the last trickle of applause. Plan ahead and arrange a late-night dessert buffet to help the evening wind down in style. Whether you are the host or an invited participant, the proper response to *"What Can I Bring?"* is "something rich and decadent!" Pull out all the stops. Now is not the time to count calories or fat grams. Help yourself to one of everything, let your senses delight in the feast before you, take a deep breath and SPLURGE!

What Can I Bring?

If your pound cake, fresh from the oven or fresh from the freezer, needs an accompaniment . . . If you find yourself without time to prepare dessert . . . If friends drop in on a coffee-mellow evening . . . In just a few moments, with these easy-to-have-on-hand garnishes, you can set up a coffee bar. Remember to make fresh pots of regular and decaf, then use your eclectic serving pieces to display these offerings and your good taste to your fortunate guests.

- *Whipped cream, sprinkled with a dash of ground cinnamon, nutmeg, cardamom, allspice, or sweetened cocoa*
- *Whipped cream, flavored with rum, almond, vanilla, chocolate, or another choice*
- *Cinnamon sticks*
- *Peppermint sticks*
- *Toffee bits*
- *Brown sugar, vanilla sugar, raw sugar*
- *Flavored syrups: we've seen cinnamon, chocolate, praline, macadamia nut, strawberry, cherry, maple . . . check your local choices*
- *Baking chips: chocolate mint, milk chocolate, white chocolate, butterscotch*
- *Broken pieces of assorted candy bars*
- *Flavored extracts: rum, almond, chocolate, vanilla*
- *Liqueurs: venture beyond the old standby, Irish, and try the hazelnut, orange, almond, coffee, peppermint . . . scan the shelves to discover new possibilities!*

For the tea lovers in your crowd, many of these accompaniments will do. Consider also,

- *Honey, available in many subtly different flavors*
- *Lemon drops*
- *Fresh mint-at your garden center, you may find chocolate, pineapple, apple, orange, and other unusual mint plants; serve them fresh, or dry in season and save for a special evening such as this*
- *Orange slices studded with cloves*

Sterling Sugar Cookies

1   cup butter or margarine, softened

1   large egg

1   teaspoon vanilla extract

½   teaspoon almond extract

1½ cups powdered sugar

1   teaspoon cream of tartar

1   teaspoon baking soda

2½ cups all-purpose flour

- Beat margarine at medium speed with an electric mixer until creamy; add egg, vanilla, and almond extract, beating well. Gradually add powdered sugar, beating well. Gradually add cream of tartar and baking soda, beating well. Add flour, ½ cup at a time, beating well after each addition.

- Chill dough 2 to 3 hours.

- Roll dough out to ¼-inch thickness on a floured surface. Cut out cookies with a cookie cutter and place on ungreased baking sheets.

- Bake at 375° for 8 to 10 minutes. Let cool completely on wire racks.

Yields 3 dozen

Dough can be prepared the day before, and stored in the refrigerator in a bowl covered with a towel.

If you bake lots of delicate cookies or cutout cookies, consider investing in reusable, nonstick silicon baking sheets. Between batches, cool baking sheets so that unbaked cookies won't melt and thin at the edges before being set by the heat of the oven.

Gingersnaps

¾   cup shortening

1   cup sugar

1   large egg

¼   cup molasses

2   cups all-purpose flour

1   tablespoon ground
      ginger

2   teaspoons baking soda

1   teaspoon ground
      cinnamon

½   teaspoon salt

- Combine first 4 ingredients in
  a mixing bowl and cream
  thoroughly.
- Combine flour and next 4 ingredients in a separate bowl. Add flour
  mixture to sugar mixture, stirring
  well.
- Roll dough into balls and roll each
  ball in sugar. Place 2 inches apart
  on baking sheets.
- Bake at 350° for 20 minutes.

Yields 3 dozen

*U*se *seasonal cookie cutters (leaves for autumn, pumpkins for Halloween, turkeys for Thanksgiving, candy canes or snowflakes for Christmas, hearts for Valentine's Day, shamrocks for St. Patrick's Day, and so on) and cut out piecrust to decorate the top crust. Baste with beaten egg white before baking for gloss.*

Sour Cream Drop Cookies

¼ cup butter or margarine, softened

1 cup sugar

1 large egg

2 cups sifted all-purpose flour

½ teaspoon baking soda

⅛ teaspoon salt

1 cup sour cream

¼ cup sugar

1½ teaspoons ground cinnamon

- Beat butter and 1 cup sugar at medium speed with an electric mixer until creamy. Add egg, beating well.

- Sift together flour, baking soda, and salt; add to butter mixture alternately with sour cream, beginning and ending with flour mixture and beating until smooth.

- Drop dough by rounded teaspoonfuls onto greased baking sheets.

- Combine ¼ cup sugar and cinnamon; sprinkle over cookies, using a shaker.

- Bake at 350° for 10 to 15 minutes.

Yields 4 dozen

Use a small ice-cream scoop to drop the dough on baking sheets, and your cookies will be more uniform in size.

Lollipop sticks, available at kitchen specialty stores, can be stuck into cookies before baking. Once they're done, "plant" your cookie flowers in foam placed in a new flowerpot. Cover the foam with Easter basket grass to complete the effect.

Peanut Butter Fingers

1	cup all-purpose flour
1	cup rolled oats
½	cup granulated sugar
½	cup firmly packed brown sugar
1	teaspoon baking soda
½	teaspoon salt
½	cup butter or margarine, melted
⅓	cup peanut butter
1	teaspoon vanilla extract
1	large egg
1	cup semisweet chocolate morsels
1	cup powdered sugar
3	tablespoons peanut butter
5	teaspoons milk

- Preheat oven to 350°.
- Combine first 10 ingredients in a large mixing bowl; pat dough into a 9 x 13 x 2-inch pan.
- Bake at 350° for 20 minutes.
- Remove from oven and sprinkle with chocolate morsels. Spread morsels over cake when melted. Let cool for 30 minutes.
- Combine powdered sugar, peanut butter, and milk; spread over chocolate. Cut into bars.

Chocoholics and peanut butter-lovers are crazy for this treat, sure to become a favorite in your family.

Chocolate Fudge Brownies

4	large eggs
2	cups sugar
1	cup all-purpose flour
1½	tablespoons vanilla extract
½	teaspoon salt
4	(1-ounce) unsweetened chocolate squares, melted
1	cup butter, melted

- Beat eggs, 1 at a time, at medium speed with an electric mixer; add sugar and beat until creamy. Add flour, vanilla, and salt, mixing well. Add melted chocolate and butter, mixing well.

- Pour batter into a greased 8 x 12-inch pan.

- Bake at 300° for 45 minutes. Let cool and serve. Delicious with vanilla ice cream and whipped cream.

Serves 8

To whip cream successfully, especially in warm weather, freeze the cream, bowl (metal is best), and whisk or beater 10 minutes before beginning whipping.

Blondie Brownies

⅓   cup unsalted butter, softened

1   cup firmly packed brown sugar

1   large egg

1   teaspoon vanilla extract

1   cup all-purpose flour

¼   teaspoon baking soda

¼   teaspoon salt

1   cup semisweet chocolate morsels

- Beat butter at medium speed with an electric mixer until creamy; gradually add brown sugar, beating well. Add egg and vanilla, beating well.

- Combine flour, baking soda, and salt; add to butter mixture, beating well. Stir in chocolate morsels. Spread batter into a greased 8-inch square pan.

- Bake at 350° for 25 minutes. Let cool on a wire rack.

- Cut into squares and store in an airtight container.

Yields 16 brownies

Because they are generally quite moist, brownies are a favorite for shipping-to college students, service personnel, or anyone away from home.

Heavenly Brownies

1	cup all-purpose flour
½	teaspoon baking powder
¼	teaspoon salt
¾	cup butter or margarine
6	tablespoons cocoa
3	medium eggs
1½	cups sugar
1	teaspoon vanilla extract
2	milk chocolate candy bars, chopped into ¼-inch pieces

- Preheat oven to 325°.

- Combine first 3 ingredients; set aside.

- Melt butter in a medium saucepan over medium heat; add cocoa and cook, stirring constantly, until chocolate sauce reaches even consistency. Remove from heat. Add eggs, stirring until blended. Add sugar, stirring until smooth. Add flour mixture, stirring until smooth. Stir in vanilla. Let cool 5 minutes. Add chocolate pieces, stirring quickly to keep from melting.

- Pour batter into an 8 x 12-inch pan lightly coated with vegetable cooking spray.

- Bake at 325° for 20 to 25 minutes or until a wooden pick inserted in center comes out clean.

Yields 15 to 20 brownies

If chocolate morsels seem to melt too much, try freezing them briefly next time.

White and Dark Brownies

¾ cup all-purpose flour

¼ teaspoon baking soda

¼ teaspoon salt

⅓ cup butter or margarine

¾ cup sugar

2 tablespoons water

1 cup semisweet chocolate
  morsels

1 tablespoon vanilla
  extract

2 large eggs

6 ounces white chocolate
  morsels, chilled

- Combine first 3 ingredients; set aside.

- Bring butter, sugar, and 2 tablespoons water to a boil in a saucepan over medium heat, stirring often. Remove from heat; stir in semisweet chocolate morsels and vanilla. Add eggs 1 at a time, beating well after each addition. Stir in flour mixture. Let cool to room temperature (about 5 minutes). Stir in chilled white chocolate morsels.

- Pour batter into a greased 8- or 9-inch square pan.

- Bake at 350° for 35 minutes.

Serves 6 to 8

Be sure to allow the mixture to cool to room temperature and use well-chilled white chocolate morsels.

Tuxedo Cups

1	(8-ounce) package cream cheese, softened
¼	teaspoon salt
1	large egg
⅓	cup sugar
1	cup semisweet chocolate morsels
1½	cups all-purpose flour
1	teaspoon baking soda
1	cup sugar
¼	cup cocoa
1	cup water
1	tablespoon vinegar
1	teaspoon vanilla extract

- Preheat oven to 350°.

- Beat first 4 ingredients at medium speed with an electric mixer until smooth. Stir in chocolate morsels; set aside.

- Beat flour and next 6 ingredients in a separate bowl at medium speed with an electric mixer. Place 1 tablespoon chocolate mixture in the bottom of each paper-lined miniature muffin pan cup. Top with 1 teaspoon cream cheese mixture.

- Bake at 350° for 20 minutes or until centers spring back when touched.

Yields 48 miniature muffins

For a special touch of color, top each tart with a perfect raspberry or small strawberry.

Lemon Fluff Pudding

3   tablespoons butter, softened

1   cup sugar, divided

¼   cup all-purpose flour

3   large eggs, separated

2   teaspoons grated lemon rind

¼   cup fresh lemon juice

1½ cups milk

¼   teaspoon salt

- Preheat oven to 325°.

- Beat butter, ½ cup sugar, and flour at medium speed with an electric mixer until creamy. Add egg yolks, beating well. Stir in lemon rind, juice, and milk.

- Beat salt and egg whites in a separate bowl at medium speed with an electric mixer until stiff peaks form. Beat in remaining ½ cup sugar. Fold egg white mixture into butter mixture.

- Pour batter into a greased 1½-quart pan.

- Bake pan in a 1-inch water bath at 325° for 1 hour. Let cool on a wire rack.

- Serve with whipped cream, if desired.

Serves 4 to 6

*C*alled *bain marie in French, the water bath technique helps assure that delicate sauces, custards, puddings, and the like don't curdle or fall apart. Place your cooking container in a large, shallow pan of warm water. This wraps your food in a warm, gentle heat. If you are uneasy about adding or removing a pan of heated water from the oven, use a turkey baster to add or remove water.*

Tiramisu

1   (3-ounce) package
    vanilla pudding (not
    instant)
2   cups milk
8   ounces mascarpone
    cheese
3   cups whipping cream
½   cup sugar
2   teaspoons vanilla extract
½   cup brewed coffee
¼   cup brandy
¼   cup Kahlúa
2   packages plain
    ladyfingers, halved
    Sweetened cocoa

- Bring pudding and milk to a boil in a saucepan; remove from heat and let cool. Add mascarpone cheese to pudding, beating at low speed with a hand-held mixer.

- Beat whipping cream, sugar, and vanilla in a separate bowl at medium speed with an electric mixer until stiff peaks form. Fold 1¾ to 2 cups whipped cream into pudding mixture. Chill.

- Combine coffee, brandy, and Kahlúa. Brush inside of each half of ladyfingers with coffee mixture.

- Line bottom and sides of a 3-quart trifle dish with ladyfingers. Pour half of pudding mixture over ladyfingers and sprinkle with sifted cocoa. Repeat layers once. Cover and chill 8 hours.

- Before serving, spread remaining whipped cream on top and sprinkle with sifted cocoa.

Serves 16 to 20

Translated "carry me up," tiramisu will make you feel you're in heaven! Serve this light and luscious dish in a sparkling trifle bowl to highlight the beauty of the ingredients. Also, be sure to chill 8 hours to allow the flavors to mingle.

Frozen Lime Torte
with Blackberry Sauce and Fresh Fruit

1   cup walnuts, toasted

1   cup almonds, toasted

⅓   cup firmly packed brown sugar

2½ teaspoons grated lime rind, divided

3   tablespoons butter or margarine, melted

1   cup granulated sugar, divided

⅓   cup plus 2 tablespoons milk

4   egg yolks

⅓   cup fresh lime juice

3   ounces white chocolate

2   cups chilled whipping cream

1   (16-ounce) package frozen blackberries, thawed

⅔   cup raspberry or berry blend juice

2   cups fresh fruit (raspberries, blueberries, strawberries, mangoes, peaches, or kiwi)

Garnish: fresh mint sprigs

- Pulse first 3 ingredients and ½ teaspoon lime rind in a food processor; add butter and process until moist crumbs form. Press crumbs firmly on the sides and bottom of an 8-inch springform pan. Freeze.

- Combine remaining 2 teaspoons lime rind, ⅔ cup sugar, and next 3 ingredients in the top of a double boiler. Bring water to a boil and cook, whisking constantly, 5 minutes or until custard consistency. Remove from heat. Whisk in white chocolate until smooth. Freeze, whisking occasionally, 45 minutes or until cold and thickened.

- Beat whipping cream at medium speed with an electric mixer until stiff peaks form. Fold lime mixture into whipped cream and pour into prepared crust. Cover and freeze overnight or up to 2 days.

- Bring remaining ⅓ cup sugar, package of blackberries, and berry juice to a boil, stirring often, in a saucepan. Puree mixture in a food processor. Pour through a wire-mesh strainer, discarding solids. Chill until cold or overnight.

(Frozen Lime Torte with Blackberry Sauce and Fresh Fruit continued)

- Remove sides from springform
  pan and transfer torte to a serving
  platter. Arrange fruit on top;
  garnish, if desired, and serve with
  blackberry sauce.

Serves 8 to 10

*H*ave citrus fruits, such as lemons, oranges, and limes, at room
temperature before juicing. Give the whole fruit a good firm roll on the counter
with the heel of your hand before juicing.
Grate the lime rind for this recipe before squeezing the lime for juice.

Lemon Chess Pie

1	medium lemon
4	large eggs
2	cups sugar
½	cup butter or margarine, softened
1	unbaked 9-inch pastry shell

- Use whole lemon with rind. Cut off both ends of lemon. Slice lemon, remove seeds.

- Process first 4 ingredients in a blender or food processor until smooth, stopping to scrape down sides. Pour into pastry shell.

- Bake at 400° for 10 minutes.

- Reduce oven temperature to 350° and bake 35 to 40 minutes or until golden brown and knife inserted in center comes out clean. Serve at room temperature.

Serves 8

The simple filling of a Southern favorite-a filling of eggs, sugar, butter, and perhaps a bit of flour-is easily changed by varying ingredients. Favorite substitutions include vanilla and brown sugar for granulated sugar.

Cranberry-Apple Pie

1   (15-ounce) package refrigerated pie crust

1½ cups cranberries, coarsely chopped

1½ cups apple, peeled and chopped

¾   cup raisins

¾   cup chopped walnuts

1½ cups sugar

2   tablespoons all-purpose flour

1   teaspoon ground cinnamon

½   cup cranberry juice

1   teaspoon vanilla extract

4   tablespoons butter or margarine, cut up

- Fit 1 pie crust into a 9-inch pie plate, according to package directions.

- Toss together cranberries and next 8 ingredients; spoon into prepared pie crust. Dot with butter.

- Roll out remaining pie crust and cut into strips. Weave strips to form a lattice over fruit mixture.

- Bake at 425° for 45 minutes or until pastry is golden brown.

Serves 8

This is a wonderful dessert for Thanksgiving dinner.

Spiked Apple Pie

8 apples, peeled and thinly sliced

¼ cup lemon juice

¼ cup rum

2⅔ cups sifted all-purpose flour

2 pinches salt

1 cup shortening

6-7 tablespoons ice water

2 tablespoons all-purpose flour

⅔ cup granulated sugar

1 tablespoon ground cinnamon

Dash of ground nutmeg

2 teaspoons brown sugar

Milk

Granulated sugar

- Combine first 3 ingredients, stirring to coat; chill.

- Combine flour and salt; cut in shortening with a pastry blender until mixture is crumbly. Add water 1 tablespoon at a time, stirring with a fork. Work dough into 2 balls using your hands; chill.

- Drain apple mixture, and return ¼ cup liquid to apple mixture. Stir in flour and next 4 ingredients; chill.

- Press 1 dough portion into a flat circle with smooth edges, using your hands. Roll dough to a circle 1½ inches larger than inverted pie plate on a lightly floured surface. Fit into pie plate, trimming edges and rolling dough to make a double thickness around rim. Flute edges, using your fingers. Prick bottom and sides with a fork.

- Spoon apple mixture into prepared pie crust, forming a dome.

- Prepare remaining dough portion as above for top crust. Brush with milk and sprinkle with sugar. Cover edges with aluminum foil.

(Spiked Apple Pie continued)

- Bake on a baking sheet at 375° for 25 minutes. Remove foil and bake 20 to 25 more minutes.

Serves 8

For variety, substitute your favorite liquor to spike this pie. Try bourbon, brandy, or the like.

Cream Cheese Pie

2   (8-ounce) packages
    cream cheese, softened
2   large eggs, lightly beaten
1   tablespoon lemon juice
1   cup sugar, divided
2   teaspoons vanilla
    extract, divided
1   baked 9-inch graham
    cracker crust
1   cup sour cream

- Preheat oven to 350°.
- Beat first 3 ingredients, ¾ cup sugar, and 1 teaspoon vanilla at medium speed with an electric mixer until light and smooth. Pour into pie crust.
- Bake at 350° for 35 minutes. Let cool on a wire rack 5 minutes.
- Beat remaining ¼ cup sugar, remaining 1 teaspoon vanilla, and sour cream at medium speed with an electric mixer until smooth. Spread over pie.
- Bake at 350° for 10 minutes. Let cool to room temperature.
- Chill 4 hours or overnight.

Serves 8 to 10

*U*se technology to make your citrus fruit produce more juice. Take the fruit from the refrigerator, and microwave at HIGH. When juicing one piece, allow about 45 seconds. Increase time by about 15 seconds for each additional piece.

Nutty Fudge Pie

½ (15-ounce) package
   refrigerated pie crusts

3 large eggs

1½ cups sugar

⅓ cup all-purpose flour

⅓ cup cocoa

½ cup butter or margarine,
   melted

½ teaspoon vanilla extract

¾ cup chopped pecans

- Fit pie crust into a 9-inch tart pan with removable bottom or a 9-inch pie plate according to package directions.

- Whisk together eggs and next 5 ingredients; stir in pecans. Pour into prepared pie crust.

- Bake at 350° for 35 to 40 minutes or until set.

- Serve with ice cream or drizzle melted chocolate over top, if desired.

Serves 8

U̶se a zip-top plastic bag to melt chocolate for drizzling over the top. Microwave at HIGH in 20 to 30 second intervals until melted. Then snip a hole in 1 corner of the bag to drizzle. Drizzle randomly or in a pattern of your choice.

What Can I Bring?

Chocolate-Pecan Chess Tart

Favorite pie or tart crust

3 cups sugar

7 tablespoons cocoa

3 tablespoons all-purpose flour

1 cup milk

4 large eggs

½ cup butter or margarine, melted

1 teaspoon vanilla extract

1 cup finely chopped pecans

12 whole pecans

Whipped cream

- Preheat oven to 375°.

- Fit pie crust into a 10- or 11-inch tart pan with removable bottom.

- Whisk together sugar and next 6 ingredients (do not vary order) until smooth; whisk in chopped pecans. Pour into prepared pie crust, discarding extra filling; top with whole pecans.

- Bake at 375° for 50 to 60 minutes or until crust is browned. Let cool on a wire rack.

- Remove sides of tart pan and serve with whipped cream.

Serves 8 to 10

Cake ingredients increase in volume when they are allowed to come to room temperature before mixing.

French Silk Pie

1½ cups graham cracker crumbs, divided

¼ cup superfine sugar

6 tablespoons butter or margarine, melted

½ cup butter or margarine

¾ cup granulated sugar

2 (1-ounce) chocolate squares, melted

1 teaspoon vanilla extract

3 large eggs

2 tablespoons brandy

Whipped cream

Chocolate curls

• Combine 1¼ cups cracker crumbs, superfine sugar, and melted butter. Press into a buttered pie plate. Bake at 350° for 10 minutes. Let cool on a wire rack. Beat ½ cup butter and granulated sugar at medium speed with an electric mixer until creamy; add melted chocolate, beating well. Add vanilla and eggs, 1 at a time, beating 2 minutes after each egg. Add brandy, beating well. Pour into prepared pie crust and chill at least 5 hours. Top with whipped cream, remaining graham cracker crumb mixture, and chocolate curls.

Serves 8

For the best and prettiest chocolate curls, use white or milk chocolate, and shave with a vegetable peeler.

Harvest Apple Crisp

4   large apples, peeled and
    sliced
1   tablespoon all-purpose
    flour
2   teaspoons ground
    cinnamon
1   tablespoon granulated
    sugar
1   cup all-purpose flour
1   cup firmly packed
    brown sugar
½   cup butter or margarine,
    cut up and softened

- Preheat oven to 350°.
- Place apple slices evenly in an 8-inch square pan.
- Combine 1 tablespoon flour, cinnamon, and granulated sugar; sprinkle over apple slices.
- Combine 1 cup flour and brown sugar; cut in butter with a pastry blender until mixture resembles coarse meal. Sprinkle over apple slices.
- Bake at 350° for 20 to 25 minutes or until bubbly and browned. Serve warm with ice cream.

Reheat leftover apple crisp for a special snow-day breakfast.

Blueberry Upside-Down Cake

1½   cups fresh blueberries

⅓   cup firmly packed brown sugar

⅛   teaspoon ground cloves

1   tablespoon butter or margarine

¼   cup water

¼   cup shortening

½   teaspoon vanilla extract

½   cup granulated sugar

1   large egg, lightly beaten

¾   cup all-purpose flour

1½   teaspoons baking powder

¼   teaspoon salt

¼   cup milk

- Preheat oven to 350°.

- Simmer first 5 ingredients in a small saucepan 5 minutes, stirring often. Pour into a greased 8-inch round cake pan.

- Beat shortening, vanilla, and granulated sugar at medium speed with an electric mixer until creamy; add egg, beating well.

- Sift together flour, baking powder, and salt; add to sugar mixture alternately with milk, beginning and ending with flour mixture. Spoon batter evenly over berries.

- Bake at 350° for 40 minutes. Let cool on a wire rack. Invert onto a serving plate.

Serves 6

*W*hipped cream will keep well if you freeze individual dollops on a cookie sheet. When frozen, transfer them to an airtight container, and return to freezer. To use them, remove from freezer 10 minutes before serving.

Best-Ever Blueberry Cobbler

3	cups fresh blueberries
3	tablespoons sugar
⅓	cup orange juice
½	cup unsalted butter, softened
½	cup sugar
1	large egg
½	teaspoon vanilla extract
⅔	cup all-purpose flour
¼	teaspoon baking powder
	Pinch of salt

- Preheat oven to 375°.

- Toss together first 3 ingredients in an 8 x 8 x 2-inch baking dish.

- Beat butter and ½ cup sugar at medium speed with an electric mixer until light and fluffy. Add egg and vanilla, beating until smooth. Gradually add flour, baking powder, and salt, beating at low speed. Drop batter in small clumps over berry mixture, covering as much surface as possible.

- Bake at 375° for 35 to 40 minutes or until crust is golden brown and filling is bubbly. Let cool briefly on a wire rack.

- Serve warm with whipped cream or vanilla ice cream.

Serves 6

The silvery frost on blueberries is a sign of freshness.

Layered Lemon Cheesecake

2	cups graham cracker crumbs
⅓	cup sugar
6	tablespoons butter or margarine, melted
3	(8-ounce) packages cream cheese, softened
3	large eggs
1¾	cups sugar, divided
1	teaspoon grated lemon rind
5	tablespoons fresh lemon juice, divided
2	teaspoons vanilla extract, divided
1	pint sour cream
3	tablespoons sugar
1	tablespoon cornstarch
½	cup water

- Combine first 3 ingredients; press into the bottom and one-fourth of the way up the sides of a 10-inch springform pan. Bake at 350° for 5 minutes. Let cool on a wire rack.

- Beat cream cheese at medium speed with an electric mixer until fluffy; add eggs, 1 at a time, beating until smooth after each addition. Add 1¼ cups sugar, lemon rind, 3 tablespoons lemon juice, and 1 teaspoon vanilla, beating well. Pour into prepared pie crust.

- Bake at 350° for 35 minutes.

- Combine sour cream, ½ cup sugar, and remaining 1 teaspoon vanilla; set in a warm place.

- Remove cake from oven and gently spread with sour cream mixture.

- Bake at 350° for 12 minutes or until set. Let cool on wire rack 30 minutes.

- Bring 3 tablespoons sugar, cornstarch, ½ cup water, and remaining 2 tablespoons lemon juice to a boil in a 1-quart saucepan. Boil, stirring constantly, 3 minutes. Chill until cool but not set. Spread on top of cake. Chill overnight.

Serves 12 to 16

Pumpkin Cheesecake

1   package graham cracker crust mix

2   (8-ounce) packages cream cheese, softened

1   cup light cream

1   cup canned pumpkin

¾   cup sugar

3   tablespoons all-purpose flour

1   teaspoon ground cinnamon

½   teaspoon ground ginger

½   teaspoon ground nutmeg

¼   teaspoon salt

1½   teaspoons vanilla extract, divided

4   large eggs, separated

1   cup sour cream

1   tablespoon sugar

- Prepare pie crust according to package directions; press into a 9-inch springform pan.
- Bake at 325° for 5 minutes.
- Beat cream cheese, next 8 ingredients, 1 teaspoon vanilla, and egg yolks at medium speed with an electric mixer until smooth.
- Beat egg whites in a separate bowl at medium speed with an electric mixer until stiff peaks form. Fold egg whites into cream cheese mixture. Pour into prepared pie crust.
- Bake at 325° for 1 hour.
- Combine sour cream, 1 tablespoon sugar, and remaining ½ teaspoon vanilla; spread over cheesecake.
- Bake at 325° for 5 to 15 minutes or until set. Chill thoroughly.

Serves 12

*F*or perfect slices of cheesecake:
1) use a thin-blade knife, wiped clean and heated in very warm water between cuts or
2) use dental floss, held very taut

Crème de Menthe Chocolate Cheesecake

1½ cups chocolate wafers, crushed

¼ cup sugar

6 tablespoons butter or margarine, divided and softened

5 (1-ounce) semisweet chocolate squares

3 (8-ounce) packages cream cheese

1 cup sugar

3 large eggs

1¼ cups sour cream, divided

¼ cup green crème de menthe

2 tablespoons white crème de cacao

4 ounces sweet baking chocolate

- Combine wafer crumbs, sugar, and 4 tablespoons butter; press on bottom and 2 inches up sides of a 9-inch springform pan. Chill 15 minutes.

- Melt semisweet chocolate in the top of a double boiler over boiling water.

- Beat remaining 2 tablespoons butter, cream cheese, and sugar at medium speed with an electric mixer until creamy; add eggs, beating until smooth. Stir in melted chocolate. Stir in 1 cup sour cream, crème de menthe, and crème de cacao. Pour into prepared crust.

- Bake at 275° for 1 hour and 15 minutes. Turn off oven and leave cheesecake in the oven with door partially open, until cooled. Let cool on a wire rack to room temperature.

- Melt sweet chocolate; let cool 5 minutes. Stir in remaining ¼ cup sour cream. Spread over slightly cooled cheesecake. Chill until set.

- Remove sides of springform pan before serving.

Serves 12

*C*hocolate can be melted in the microwave; use a microwave-safe bowl that can also be your mixing bowl, and you've saved chocolate and an extra dirty bowl! Just break squares into smaller chunks and microwave at HIGH, stirring every 10 seconds, until melted.

Mocha Chocolate Cheesecake

¼   cup chocolate wafer crumbs

¼   cup sugar

¼   cup butter or margarine, melted

1   (8-ounce) package cream cheese, softened

14   ounces sweetened condensed milk

2   tablespoons instant coffee granules

1   tablespoon hot water

⅔   cup chocolate syrup

1   cup whipping cream, whipped

- Combine first 3 ingredients; press into an 8-inch springform pan. Chill.

- Beat cream cheese at medium speed with an electric mixer until fluffy; add sweetened condensed milk, beating well.

- Dissolve coffee granules in 1 tablespoon hot water. Add coffee and chocolate syrup to cream cheese mixture, beating well. Fold in whipped cream. Spoon into prepared crust.

- Freeze 6 hours.

Serves 6

This is a wonderful cake to keep on hand in the freezer. Try serving with a strawberry or raspberry sauce.

Black Russian Cake

1 (18.25-ounce) package
yellow cake mix

1 (5.1-ounce) package
instant chocolate
pudding mix

4 large eggs

1 cup vegetable oil

½ cup vodka

½ cup water

½ cup sugar

½ cup Kahlúa, divided

½ cup powdered sugar

- Beat first 7 ingredients and ¼ cup Kahlúa at medium speed with an electric mixer until smooth; pour into a greased and floured Bundt pan.

- Bake at 350° for 50 minutes.

- Combine remaining ¼ cup Kahlúa and powdered sugar, stirring until smooth. Let cake cool slightly. Remove cake from pan. Puncture cake surface with a large wooden pick and brush with glaze. Let harden.

Serves 16

This moist and easy cake works well on a buffet.

Chocolate Pound Cake

½ pound butter or
    margarine, softened
½ cup shortening
3 cups sugar
6 large eggs
3 cups all-purpose flour
½ teaspoon baking powder
¼ teaspoon salt
½ cup cocoa
1¼ cups milk
2 teaspoons vanilla extract

- Beat first 3 ingredients at medium speed with an electric mixer until creamy; add eggs, 1 at a time, beating well after each addition.

- Sift together flour and next 3 ingredients; add to creamed mixture alternately with milk, beginning and ending with flour mixture and beating constantly. Add vanilla, beating well. Pour into a greased and floured 9-inch tube pan.

- Bake at 350° for 15 minutes. Reduce oven temperature to 325° and bake 1 hour.

Yields 1 cake

Simply a classic. Serve plain, or frost, or accompany with fresh berries or peaches and whipped cream.

Almond Pound Cake

1 cup butter or margarine, softened

½ cup shortening

3 cups sugar

5 large eggs

3 cups sifted all-purpose flour

¼ teaspoon baking powder

1 cup milk

2 tablespoons almond or lemon extract

- Beat first 3 ingredients at medium speed with an electric mixer until light and fluffy. Add eggs, 1 at a time, beating well after each addition.

- Sift together flour and baking powder; add to butter mixture, beating well. Add milk, beating well. Add almond extract, beating well. Pour batter into a greased and floured 10-inch tube pan.

- Place in a cold oven. Bake at 325° for 1½ hours. Let cool in pan on a wire rack 10 minutes. Invert on a serving platter.

Serves 8

For variety, consider substituting other extracts for almond; try lemon, rum, or coconut.

Cherry Butter Cake

½   cup butter or margarine

4   large eggs, divided

1   (18.25-ounce) package yellow cake mix

1   (20-ounce) can cherry pie filling

1   (8-ounce) package cream cheese, softened

1   (16-ounce) package powdered sugar

- Melt butter in a 9 x 13 x 2-inch pan.

- Prepare cake mix according to directions on box; spoon batter evenly over butter. Spread pie filling over batter.

- Beat cream cheese and remaining 2 eggs at medium speed with an electric mixer until creamy; add powdered sugar, beating well. Spread over pie filling.

- Bake at 350° for 40 to 45 minutes or until golden brown.

Serves 5 to 7

It's easy to have most of these ingredients in the cupboard for a quick fix on the spur of the moment.

Chocolate-Nut Loaf Cake

1½ cups sifted all-purpose flour

¾ teaspoon baking soda

½ teaspoon salt

⅓ cup butter or margarine, softened

¾ cup sugar

1 large egg

1 teaspoon vanilla extract

2 (1-ounce) unsweetened chocolate squares, melted

¾ cup buttermilk

½ cup nuts, chopped

- Sift together first 3 ingredients.
- Beat butter at medium speed with an electric mixer until creamy; gradually add sugar, beating well after each addition until light and fluffy. Add egg and vanilla, beating well. Add chocolate, beating well. Add flour mixture alternately with buttermilk, beginning and ending with flour mixture and beating until smooth after each addition. Stir in nuts. Spoon into a greased 8 x 8 x 2-inch pan.
- Bake at 350° for 35 to 45 minutes.

Serves 6 to 8

𝒩uts can be chopped quickly and easily if the pieces are placed in a zip-top plastic bag with air pressed out before sealing. Then take out your frustrations and pound the bag several times with a meat mallet.

What Can I Bring?

Chain Bridge Chocolate Cake

2	cups all-purpose flour
2	cups sugar
2	large eggs
½	cup sour cream
½	teaspoon salt
1	teaspoon baking soda
1	cup butter or margarine
¼	cup cocoa
1	cup water
	Chocolate Icing

- Preheat oven to 350°.
- Beat first 6 ingredients at medium speed with an electric mixer until smooth.
- Bring butter, cocoa, and 1 cup water to a boil in a small saucepan; add to flour mixture, beating at low speed until well blended. Pour into a greased and floured 10 x 15-inch jelly-roll pan.
- Bake at 350° for 20 minutes.
- Spread warm cake with Chocolate Icing.

Serves 12 to 16

Chocolate Icing

4	teaspoons cocoa
½	cup butter
2	tablespoons milk
1	(16-ounce) package powdered sugar
1	teaspoon vanilla extract
1	cup pecans, finely chopped

- Bring first 3 ingredients to a boil in a small saucepan. Whisk in powdered sugar, vanilla, and pecans, until icing consistency. Spread while hot.

A perfect treat for a crowd, but be sure all your ingredients are measured and ready, to insure against interruptions while preparing this cake.

Hot Chocolate Sauce

6   (1-ounce) chocolate
      squares
2   cups sugar
½   cup butter
      Pinch of salt
1   (12-ounce) can
      evaporated milk
1   teaspoon vanilla extract

- Melt chocolate in a saucepan over medium-low heat, stirring constantly. Add sugar, butter, and salt and bring to a boil. Boil several minutes. Add milk and return to a boil. Add vanilla, stirring well.

- Serve sauce hot. Refrigerate unused portion and reheat to serve again.

Serves 8 to 10

This good, thick sauce, delicious over ice cream, can be made quickly from ingredients you're sure to have on hand.

Roasted Banana Sauce

12 ripe bananas, cut into chunks

¾ cup butter

2 teaspoons ground cinnamon

1 cup brown sugar, packed

2 teaspoons vanilla extract

- Combine all ingredients in a large roasting pan; cover with aluminum foil.

- Bake at 350° for 20 to 30 minutes or until banana has completely broken down. Let cool at room temperature.

- Mash with a spoon until desired consistency, adding 2 tablespoons water if mixture is too thick. Serve at room temperature. Do not refrigerate.

Serves 12 to 20

Serve this yummy sauce over ice cream or cake. It's especially good over chocolate cake.

Chocolate-Peanut Clusters

2	tablespoons peanut butter
6	ounces butterscotch morsels
1	cup semisweet chocolate morsels
2	cups salted Spanish peanuts

- Cook first 3 ingredients in a heavy saucepan over low heat, stirring constantly, until melted. Stir in peanuts.
- Drop by rounded spoonfuls onto wax paper. Chill until firm.
- Place in an airtight container and chill.

Yields 4 dozen

You can also melt first 3 ingredients in the microwave in a microwave-safe dish, stirring frequently.

During warm weather, protect these clusters from the heat. When storing, keep refrigerated until ready to serve. Also, serve carefully, keeping remainders refrigerated between replenishing your platters.

Crispy Caramel Corn

2   cups firmly packed
    brown sugar
1   cup butter or margarine
½   cup light corn syrup
1   tablespoon vanilla
    extract
1   teaspoon salt
½   teaspoon baking soda
2   cups chopped nuts
    (optional)
28 cups popped corn or
    1½ cups raw popcorn,
    popped

- Cook first 3 ingredients in a
  1½-quart saucepan over medium
  heat, stirring occasionally,
  5 minutes. Remove from heat,
  and stir in vanilla. Add salt and
  baking soda. Beat with a hand-
  held mixer until frothy.

- Pour caramel mixture and, if
  desired, nuts over popcorn. Mix
  thoroughly. Spread on greased
  baking sheets.

- Bake at 250° for 1 hour, stirring
  every 15 minutes.

- Remove from oven and let cool,
  stirring occasionally.

Serves 18 to 20

The baking step is the key to this extra crispy treat.

Index

A

All-Purpose Marinade
(for Chicken, Shrimp, or Tofu) 99
Almond Pound Cake 265

Appetizers (see also Dips & Spreads)
Antipasto 10
Crab Melt-a-Ways 27
Crostini with Toppers 12
Festive Pepper Cheesecake 8
Flank Steak Appetizer 25
Gravlax 32
Kingstowne Wraps 38
Mushroom Canapés 14
Parmesan-Herb Almonds 40
Party Pecans 41
Patio Shrimp 30
Puff Pastry Pizza with
Onions and Carrots 11
Roasted Vegetable Canapés 16
Smoked Salmon Pinwheels 31
Spicy Marinated Shrimp 29
Tomato Company Cups 21

Apples
Apple Muffins 161
Apple Noodle Pudding 174
Cranberry-Apple Pie 249
Harvest Apple Crisp 256
Spiked Apple Pie 250
Arlington Almond Chicken 71

Artichokes
Clifton Day Pasta 133
Pollo Saltimbocca 56
Sherried Artichoke Chicken 58
Ashburn Chicken 70

Asparagus
Asparagus with
Mustard-Yogurt Sauce 187
Bow-Tie Pasta with Asparagus
in Lemon Cream Sauce 126
Festive Asparagus 186
Sausage and Roasted
Vegetable Couscous 138

Avocados
Black Bean Salsa 35
Papaya Salad 214
Roasted Corn Guacamole 34

B

B-B-Q Sauce 53
Baked Rice Pilaf 211

Bananas
Banana-Chocolate
Chip Nut Bread 155
Roasted Banana Sauce 270
Barbecued Short Ribs 50
Barley-Vegetable Soup 114

Beans
Bean Sprout Salad 226
Black Bean Enchiladas 142
Black Bean Hummus 36
Black Bean Salsa 35
Calico Bean Casserole 145
Cheddar-Green
Bean Casserole 189
Garbanzo, Feta,
and Olive Salad 224
Hearty Chili 110
Key Lime Pasta
with Black Beans 128
Lentil Salad 223
Oven-Roasted Vegetables 204
Reston Veggie Salad 221
Spectacular Platter 184
Tavern Tortilla Soup 109
Tortilla-Black Bean Casserole 135
Veggie and Bean Quesadillas 140
White Chili 105

Beef
Barbecued Short Ribs 50
Beef Burgundy 49
Beef Godunov 51
Burgundy Beef Stew 115
Calico Bean Casserole 145
Chilled Oriental Beef Salad 147

What Can I Bring?

Fabulous Fajitas 139
Flank Steak Appetizer 25
Grilled Flank Steak 55
Hearty Chili 110
Hot Reuben Dip 24
Marinated Beef Tenderloin 54
Pulled Beef Sandwiches 136
Spicy Tortilla Casserole 144
Stuffed Flank Steak 48
Tailgate Brisket 52
Veal Scaloppine 97
White Lasagna 127
Zucchini Enchiladas 141
Best-Ever Blueberry Cobbler 258

Beverages
Bride's Punch 42
Celebration Mint Tea 43
Coffee Liqueur Smoothie 46
Holiday Cider 44
Holiday Irish Coffee Eggnog 43
Hot Ruby Apple Drink 45
Black Bean Enchiladas 142
Black Bean Hummus 36
Black Bean Salsa 35
Blackberry Sauce and Fresh Fruit,
Frozen Lime Torte with 246
Black Russian Cake 263
Black-Eyed Pea Dip 37
Blondie Brownies 240
Blue Cheese-Potato Salad 219

Blueberries
Best-Ever Blueberry Cobbler 258
Blueberry Upside-Down Cake .. 257
Delicious Blueberry Muffins 160
Bow-Tie Pasta with Asparagus
in Lemon Cream Sauce 126

Breads
Apple Muffins 161
Banana-Chocolate
Chip Nut Bread 155
Cranberry Bread 158
Crystal City Coffee Cake 162
Dark Zucchini Bread 157
Delicious Blueberry Muffins 160

Orange-Poppy Seed Bread 154
Pumpkin Bread 156
Refrigerator Rolls 163
Sweet Potato Rolls 164
Vienna Breakfast Muffins 159
Bride's Punch 42

Broccoli
Easy Broccoli Soup 108
Spectacular Platter 184
Summer Veggie Pasta Salad 225
Vegetable Stir-Fry
with Ginger Sauce 148
Veggie and Bean Quesadillas 140
Walnut Broccoli 183

Brunches
Apple Noodle Pudding 174
Brunch Casserole 172
Cinnamon-Raisin
Breakfast Pudding 175
Franklin Farms French Toast 176
Fruited Sausage Casserole 170
Garden Fresh Frittata 168
Garlic-Cheese Grits 173
Grape Salad 178
Heavenly Pancakes 177
Hospitality Casserole 180
Salmon Quiche 166
Sausage and Salsa Casserole 171
Strawberries Excellent 179
Tomato and Onion Tart 169
Vegetable Quiche 167
Burgundy Beef Stew 115

C

Cabbage
Crunchy Chicken
Chopped Salad 217
Kingstowne Wraps 38
Picnic Slaw 229
Vegetable Stir-Fry
with Ginger Sauce 148
Cajun Chicken
and Shrimp Over Pasta 93

Index

Cakes

Almond Pound Cake 265
Black Russian Cake 263
Blueberry Upside-Down Cake .. 257
Chain Bridge Chocolate Cake 268
Cherry Butter Cake 266
Chocolate Pound Cake 264
Chocolate-Nut Loaf Cake 267
Calico Bean Casserole 145

Carrots

Barley-Vegetable Soup 114
Carrot Ambrosia Salad 213
Cream of Carrot
    and Lemon Soup 104
Crystal Glazed Carrots 188
Garden Fresh Frittata 168
Puff Pastry Pizza
    with Onions and Carrots 11
Sausage and Roasted
    Vegetable Couscous 138
Vegetable Stir-Fry
    with Ginger Sauce 148
Winter Vegetable Soup 106
Cascades Potato Salad 220

Casseroles

Apple Noodle Pudding 174
Baked Rice Pilaf 211
Black Bean Enchiladas 142
Brunch Casserole 172
Calico Bean Casserole 145
Cheddar-Green
    Bean Casserole 189
Cheesy Scalloped Potatoes 203
Chicken Tetrazzini 64
Cinnamon-Raisin
    Breakfast Pudding 175
Confetti Rice 212
Crab Imperial 90
Eggplant-Tomato Casserole 191
Fresh Tomato-Basil Casserole 194
Fruited Sausage Casserole 170
Garden Fresh Frittata 168
Garlic-Cheese Grits 173
Great Falls Potatoes 202

Green Chile Lasagna 151
Holiday Sweet Potatoes 198
Hospitality Casserole 180
Potomac Falls Polenta 208
Pumpkin Puff 197
Salmon Quiche 166
Sausage and Salsa Casserole 171
Seafood Lasagna 84
Southern Corn Pudding 196
Spicy Tortilla Casserole 144
Sweet Potato Casserole 199
Tomato and Onion Tart 169
Tomato Pie 190
Tortilla-Black Bean Casserole 135
Vegetable Quiche 167
Vidalia Onion
    and Rice Casserole 210
Walnut Broccoli 183
White Lasagna 127
Zesty Stuffed Zucchini 195
Zucchini Enchiladas 141
Celebration Mint Tea 43
Chain Bridge Chocolate Cake 268
Chantilly Crab Dip 26
Cheddar-Green Bean Casserole 189

Cheese

Antipasto 10
Black-Eyed Pea Dip 37
Blue Cheese-Potato Salad 219
Brunch Casserole 172
Cheddar-Green
    Bean Casserole 189
Cheesy Scalloped Potatoes 203
Confetti Rice 212
Crab Melt-a-Ways 27
Crostini with Toppers 12
Feta Shrimp 94
Garbanzo, Feta,
    and Olive Salad 224
Garlic-Cheese Grits 173
Gold Cup Cheese Spread 18
Green Chile Lasagna 151
Grilled Eggplant and
    Goat Cheese Salad 132
Hearts of Palm Dip 20

What Can I Bring?

Hospitality Casserole 180
Hot Reuben Dip 24
Mandarin Blue Spinach Salad ... 215
Potomac Falls Polenta 208
Puff Pastry Pizza
   with Onions and Carrots 11
Spicy Tortilla Casserole 144
Spinach and Feta Pizza 150
Three-Cheese Ravioli 125
Tortilla-Black Bean Casserole 135
Virginia Country Ham Spread 23
White Lasagna 127
Zucchini Enchiladas 141
Cherry Butter Cake 266

Chicken
Arlington Almond Chicken 71
Ashburn Chicken 70
Cajun Chicken and
   Shrimp Over Pasta 93
Chicken Breasts Lombardy 65
Chicken Marsala 67
Chicken Tetrazzini 64
Chicken with Fruit Salsa 63
Clifton Day Pasta 133
Coconut-Chicken Soup 120
Crisp and Tangy Chicken 72
Crunchy Chicken
   Chopped Salad 217
Cumin Chicken
   with Hot Citrus Salsa 60
Green Chile Lasagna 151
Honey-Mustard Chicken 69
Lite and Spicy Peanut
   and Chicken Pasta 62
Marinated Chicken Breasts 66
Pesto Grilled Chicken 68
Plum Chicken with Snow Peas 61
Pollo Saltimbocca 56
Roast Chicken
   with Orange-Port Sauce 57
Sherried Artichoke Chicken 58
Spicy Chicken
   with Peanut Sauce 59
Tarragon Chicken Salad 216

Virginia Bicentennial
   Chicken Salad 146
White Chili 105
Chilled Oriental Beef Salad 147
Chilled Tortellini Salad 131

Chocolate
Banana-Chocolate
   Chip Nut Bread 155
Black Russian Cake 263
Blondie Brownies 240
Chain Bridge Chocolate Cake 268
Chocolate Fudge Brownies 239
Chocolate Icing 268
Chocolate Pound Cake 264
Chocolate-Nut Loaf Cake 267
Chocolate-Peanut Clusters 271
Chocolate-Pecan Chess Tart 254
Crème de Menthe Chocolate
   Cheesecake 261
French Silk Pie 255
Frozen Lime Torte with
   Blackberry Sauce
   and Fresh Fruit 246
Heavenly Brownies 241
Hot Chocolate Sauce 269
Mocha Chocolate Cheesecake 262
Nutty Fudge Pie 253
Peanut Butter Fingers 238
Tuxedo Cups 243
White and Dark Brownies 242
Chutney Cheese Ball 39
Cinnamon-Raisin
   Breakfast Pudding 175
Clifton Day Pasta 133
Coconut
   Carrot Ambrosia Salad 213
   Coconut-Chicken Soup 120
Coffee Liqueur Smoothie 46

Condiments & Relishes
All-Purpose Marinade (for
   Chicken, Shrimp, or Tofu) 99
B-B-Q Sauce 53
Cranberry-Horseradish Relish.... 228

Creole Sauce 83
Curry-Almond Dressing 232
Enchilada Sauce 143
Ginger Sauce 149
Marinade for Beef or Chicken 98
Mustard Sauce 73
Sauce for Ham 100
Summer Tomato Dressing 231
Tomato-Basil Vinaigrette
    for Pasta 122
Yogurt-Dill Sauce 87
Zesty Herb Dressing 185
Confetti Rice 212

Cookies & Bars
Blondie Brownies........................... 240
Chocolate Fudge Brownies 239
Gingersnaps 236
Heavenly Brownies 241
Peanut Butter Fingers 238
Sour Cream Drop Cookies 237
Sterling Sugar Cookies................ 235
White and Dark Brownies 242

Corn
Black Bean Salsa............................. 35
Halftime Hot and
    Spicy Corn Dip 33
Hunt Club Corn Chowder 118
Middleburg Medley 182
Reston Veggie Salad 221
Roasted Corn Guacamole 34
Southern Corn Pudding 196
Veggie and Bean Quesadillas 140

Couscous
Couscous Amandine 152
Sausage and Roasted
    Vegetable Couscous 138
Crab Cakes with Creole Sauce 82
Crab Imperial 90
Crab Melt-a-Ways 27

Cranberries
Cranberry Bread 158
Cranberry-Apple Pie 249

Cranberry-Horseradish
    Relish 228
Cream Cheese Pie 252
Cream of Carrot
    and Lemon Soup 104
Creamy Salmon Fettuccine 129
Creamy Tomato-Sausage
    Sauce with Shells......................... 134
Crème de Menthe
    Chocolate Cheesecake 261
Creole Sauce 83
Crisp and Tangy Chicken 72
Crispy Caramel Corn 272
Crostini with Toppers 12
Crunchy Chicken
    Chopped Salad 217
Crystal City Coffee Cake 162
Crystal Glazed Carrots 188
Cumin Chicken
    with Hot Citrus Salsa 60
Curry-Almond Dressing................. 232

D

Dark Zucchini Bread 157
Delicious Blueberry Muffins 160

Desserts (see also Cakes, Chocolate,
Cookies & Bars, and Pies)
Best-Ever Blueberry Cobbler 258
Chocolate-Peanut Clusters 271
Crème de Menthe Chocolate
    Cheesecake 261
Crispy Caramel Corn 272
Frozen Lime Torte with
    Blackberry Sauce
    and Fresh Fruit 246
Harvest Apple Crisp 256
Hot Chocolate Sauce 269
Layered Lemon Cheesecake 259
Lemon Fluff Pudding.................. 244
Mocha Chocolate Cheesecake 262
Pumpkin Cheesecake 260
Roasted Banana Sauce 270
Tiramisu 245
Tuxedo Cups 243

What Can I Bring?

Dips & Spreads

Black Bean Hummus 36
Black Bean Salsa 35
Black-Eyed Pea Dip 37
Chantilly Crab Dip 26
Chutney Cheese Ball 39
Elegant Layered Torta 9
Gold Cup Cheese Spread 18
Halftime Hot and
    Spicy Corn Dip 33
Hearts of Palm Dip 20
Hot Reuben Dip 24
Lemon-Tuna Mousse 28
Roasted Corn Guacamole 34
Roasted Red Pepper Dip 17
Sassy Sausage Dip 22
Sun-Dried Tomato Spread 19
Virginia Country Ham Spread 23

E

Easy Apple-Glazed Pork Chops 77
Easy Broccoli Soup 108

Eggplant

Eggplant-Tomato Casserole 191
Grilled Eggplant and
    Goat Cheese Salad 132
Oven-Roasted Vegetables 204
Roasted Eggplant Risotto 205
Roasted Vegetable Canapés 16
Elegant Layered Torta 9
Enchilada Sauce 143
Endive with Hot Bacon Dressing ... 230

F

Fabulous Fajitas 139
Fair Lakes Mushrooms 192
Fairfax Station Shrimp
    Over Fettuccine 92
Festive Asparagus 186
Festive Pepper Cheesecake 8
Feta Shrimp 94

Fish

Salmon

Creamy Salmon Fettuccine 129
Gravlax 32
Lime Broiled Salmon Steaks 88
Salmon Quiche 166
Salmon Wellington 86
Salmon with
    Yogurt-Dill Sauce 87
Smoked Salmon Pinwheels 31

Tuna

Grilled Pepper Tuna with
    Cilantro Butter 81
Lemon-Tuna Mousse 28

White Fish

Pecan-Crusted Fish 95
Flank Steak Appetizer 25
Franklin Farms French Toast 176
French Onion Soup 103
French Silk Pie 255
Fresh Tomato-Basil Casserole 194

Frostings & Icings

Chocolate Icing 268
Orange Glaze 154
Frozen Lime Torte with
    Blackberry Sauce
    and Fresh Fruit 246
Fruited Sausage Casserole 170

G

Garbanzo, Feta, and Olive Salad ... 224
Garden Fresh Frittata 168
Garlic Mashed Potatoes 200
Garlic-Cheese Grits 173
Ginger Pork Steaks 74
Ginger Sauce 149
Gingersnaps 236
Gold Cup Cheese Spread 18

Grapes

Grape Salad 178
Virginia Bicentennial
    Chicken Salad 146

Gravlax 32
Great Falls Potatoes 202
Green Chile Lasagna 151
Grilled Eggplant and
    Goat Cheese Salad 132
Grilled Flank Steak 55
Grilled Garlic Shrimp 89
Grilled Pepper Tuna
    with Cilantro Butter 81
Grilled Portobello
    Mushroom Slices 207

Grits
    Garlic-Cheese Grits 173
    Potomac Falls Polenta 208

H

Halftime Hot and
    Spicy Corn Dip 33
Harvest Apple Crisp 256

Hearts of Palm
    Hearts of Palm Dip 20
    Smoked Salmon Pinwheels 31
Hearty Chili 110
Heavenly Brownies 241
Heavenly Pancakes 177
Herbed Baby Red Potatoes 201
Holiday Cider 44
Holiday Irish Coffee Eggnog 43
Holiday Sweet Potatoes 198
Honey-Mustard Chicken 69
Hospitality Casserole 180
Hot Chocolate Sauce 269
Hot Reuben Dip 24
Hot Ruby Apple Drink 45
Hunt Club Corn Chowder 118

K

Key Lime Pasta
    with Black Beans 128
Kingstowne Wraps 38

L

Lamb Chops, Rosemary 96
Layered Lemon Cheesecake 259
Lemon Chess Pie 248
Lemon Fluff Pudding 244
Lemon-Tuna Mousse 28
Lentil Salad 223
Lime Broiled Salmon Steaks 88
Lite and Spicy Peanut
    and Chicken Pasta 62

M

Mandarin Blue Spinach Salad 215
Marinade for Beef or Chicken 98
Marinated Beef Tenderloin 54
Marinated Chicken Breasts 66
Marinated Pork Tenderloin
    with Dried Fruit 75
Marinated Pork Tenderloin
    with Mustard Sauce 73
Middleburg Medley 182
Mocha Chocolate Cheesecake 262

Mushrooms
    Barley-Vegetable Soup 114
    Beef Burgundy 49
    Beef Godunov 51
    Chicken Tetrazzini 64
    Clifton Day Pasta 133
    Crostini with Toppers 12
    Fair Lakes Mushrooms 192
    Grilled Portobello
        Mushroom Slices 207
    Mushroom Canapés 14
    Mushrooms with a Kick 193
    Pasta with Sausage, Leeks,
        and Mushrooms 123
    Portobello Mushroom Risotto
        with Feta Cheese 206
    Sherried Artichoke Chicken 58
    Spectacular Platter 184

What Can I Bring?

Veal Scaloppine 97
Winter Vegetable Soup 106
Mustard Sauce 73

N

Northern Neck Crab Cakes 91

Nuts
Almond Pound Cake 265
Arlington Almond Chicken 71
Banana-Chocolate
   Chip Nut Bread 155
Chocolate-Nut Loaf Cake 267
Chocolate-Peanut Clusters 271
Chocolate-Pecan Chess Tart 254
Couscous Amandine 152
Crispy Caramel Corn 272
Curry-Almond Dressing 232
Frozen Lime Torte with
   Blackberry Sauce
   and Fresh Fruit 246
Nutty Fudge Pie 253
Parmesan-Herb Almonds 40
Party Pecans 41
Pecan-Crusted Fish 95
Walnut Broccoli 183

O

Old Town Alexandria
   Crab Soup 113

Onions
French Onion Soup 103
Puff Pastry Pizza with
   Onions and Carrots 11
Roasted Vegetable Canapés 16
Simmered Onions 137
Tomato and Onion Tart 169
Vegetable Quiche 167
Vidalia Onion and
   Rice Casserole 210
Winter Vegetable Soup 106
Orange Glaze 154
Orange-Poppy Seed Bread 154

Oranges
Carrot Ambrosia Salad 213
Cumin Chicken
   with Hot Citrus Salsa 60
Mandarin Blue Spinach Salad ... 215
Oven-Roasted Vegetables 204

P

Papaya Salad 214
Parmesan-Herb Almonds 40
Party Pecans 41

Pasta
Apple Noodle Pudding 174
Beef Godunov 51
Bow-Tie Pasta with Asparagus
   in Lemon Cream Sauce 126
Cajun Chicken and Shrimp
   Over Pasta 93
Chicken Tetrazzini 64
Chilled Tortellini Salad 131
Clifton Day Pasta 133
Creamy Salmon Fettuccine 129
Creamy Tomato-Sausage
   Sauce with Shells 134
Fairfax Station Shrimp
   Over Fettuccine 92
Green Chile Lasagna 151
Key Lime Pasta
   with Black Beans 128
Lite and Spicy Peanut
   and Chicken Pasta 62
Pasta with Prosciutto 124
Pasta with Sausage, Leeks,
   and Mushrooms 123
Potomac Pork Pasta 130
Seafood Lasagna 84
Summer Veggie Pasta Salad 225
Three-Cheese Ravioli 125
White Lasagna 127
Patio Shrimp 30

Peaches
Chicken with Fruit Salsa 63

Index

Frozen Lime Torte with
Blackberry Sauce and
Fresh Fruit 246
Fruited Sausage Casserole 170
Peanut Butter Fingers 238

Peas

Black-Eyed Pea Dip 37
Plum Chicken with Snow Peas 61
Reston Veggie Salad 221
Tantalizing Pea Salad 227
Pecan-Crusted Fish 95
Pesto Grilled Chicken 68
Picnic Slaw 229

Pies

Chocolate-Pecan Chess Tart 254
Cranberry-Apple Pie 249
Cream Cheese Pie 252
French Silk Pie 255
Lemon Chess Pie 248
Nutty Fudge Pie 253
Spiked Apple Pie 250
Pine Nut and Olive Rice Salad 222

Pineapple

Hospitality Casserole 180
Virginia Bicentennial
Chicken Salad 146
Pizza Soup 112
Plum Chicken with Snow Peas 61
Pollo Saltimbocca 56

Pork

Antipasto 10
Brunch Casserole 172
Calico Bean Casserole 145
Creamy Tomato-Sausage
Sauce with Shells 134
Easy Apple-Glazed
Pork Chops 77
Endive with
Hot Bacon Dressing 230
Fruited Sausage Casserole 170
Ginger Pork Steaks 74
Marinated Pork Tenderloin
with Dried Fruit 75

Marinated Pork Tenderloin
with Mustard Sauce 73
Pasta with Prosciutto 124
Pasta with Sausage, Leeks,
and Mushrooms 123
Pizza Soup 112
Pork Tenderloin Stuffed
with Dried Fruit 80
Potomac Pork Pasta 130
Roast Pork Calypso 78
Sassy Sausage Dip 22
Sausage and Salsa Casserole 171
Spareribs 76
Tangy Fruit Pork Chops 79
Virginia Country Ham Spread 23
Waterfront Gumbo 116
White Lasagna 127
Portobello Mushroom Risotto
with Feta Cheese 206

Potatoes

Barley-Vegetable Soup 114
Blue Cheese-Potato Salad 219
Cascades Potato Salad 220
Cheesy Scalloped Potatoes 203
Garlic Mashed Potatoes 200
Great Falls Potatoes 202
Herbed Baby Red Potatoes 201
Oven-Roasted Vegetables 204
Potato Salad with
Horseradish-Dill Sauce 218
Roasted Garlic
and Potato Soup 117
Sausage and Roasted
Vegetable Couscous 138
Winter Vegetable Soup 106
Potomac Falls Polenta 208
Potomac Pork Pasta 130
Puff Pastry Pizza with
Onions and Carrots 11
Pulled Beef Sandwiches 136

Pumpkin

Pumpkin Bread 156
Pumpkin Cheesecake 260
Pumpkin Puff 197

What Can I Bring?

R

Refrigerator Rolls 163
Reston Veggie Salad 221

Rice

Baked Rice Pilaf 211
Beef Godunov 51
Chicken Marsala 67
Confetti Rice 212
Cumin Chicken with
   Hot Citrus Salsa 60
Feta Shrimp 94
Pine Nut and Olive
   Rice Salad 222
Plum Chicken with Snow Peas 61
Portobello Mushroom
   Risotto with Feta Cheese 206
Roasted Eggplant Risotto 205
Seasoned Basmati Rice 209
Shrimp Jambalaya 107
Spicy Chicken
   with Peanut Sauce 59
Vidalia Onion
   and Rice Casserole 210
Waterfront Gumbo 116
Roast Chicken
   with Orange-Port Sauce 57
Roast Pork Calypso 78
Roasted Banana Sauce 270
Roasted Corn Guacamole 34
Roasted Eggplant Risotto 205
Roasted Garlic and Potato Soup 117
Roasted Red Pepper Dip 17
Roasted Vegetable Canapés 16
Rosemary Lamb Chops 96

S

Salads

Bean Sprout Salad 226
Blue Cheese-Potato Salad 219
Carrot Ambrosia Salad 213
Cascades Potato Salad 220
Chilled Oriental Beef Salad 147
Chilled Tortellini Salad 131
Crunchy Chicken
   Chopped Salad 217
Endive with
   Hot Bacon Dressing 230
Garbanzo, Feta,
   and Olive Salad 224
Grape Salad 178
Grilled Eggplant
   and Goat Cheese Salad 132
Lentil Salad 223
Mandarin Blue Spinach Salad ... 215
Papaya Salad 214
Picnic Slaw 229
Pine Nut and
   Olive Rice Salad 222
Potato Salad with
   Horseradish-Dill Sauce 218
Reston Veggie Salad 221
Summer Veggie Pasta Salad 225
Tantalizing Pea Salad 227
Tarragon Chicken Salad 216
Tomato and Basil Salad 228
Virginia Bicentennial
   Chicken Salad 146
Salmon Quiche 166
Salmon Wellington 86
Salmon with Yogurt-Dill Sauce 87
Sandwiches, Pulled Beef 136
Sassy Sausage Dip 22
Sauce for Ham 100
Sausage and Roasted
   Vegetable Couscous 138
Sausage and Salsa Casserole 171

Seafood

Crab
   Chantilly Crab Dip 26
   Crab Cakes
      with Creole Sauce 82
   Crab Imperial 90
   Crab Melt-a-Ways 27
   Northern Neck Crab Cakes 91
   Old Town Alexandria
      Crab Soup 113

Index

Seafood Lasagna 84
Scallops
   Simply Sensational Scallops 85
Shrimp
   Cajun Chicken and
     Shrimp Over Pasta 93
   Clifton Day Pasta 133
   Fairfax Station Shrimp
     Over Fettuccine 92
   Feta Shrimp 94
   Grilled Garlic Shrimp 89
   Patio Shrimp 30
   Seafood Lasagna 84
   Shrimp Jambalaya 107
   Spicy Marinated Shrimp 29
   Waterfront Gumbo 116
Seasoned Basmati Rice 209
Sherried Artichoke Chicken 58
Simmered Onions 137
Simply Sensational Scallops 85
Smoked Salmon Pinwheels 31

Soups and Stews
   Barley-Vegetable Soup 114
   Burgundy Beef Stew 115
   Coconut-Chicken Soup 120
   Cream of Carrot
     and Lemon Soup 104
   Easy Broccoli Soup 108
   French Onion Soup 103
   Hearty Chili 110
   Hunt Club Corn Chowder 118
   Old Town Alexandria
     Crab Soup 113
   Pizza Soup 112
   Roasted Garlic
     and Potato Soup 117
   Shrimp Jambalaya 107
   Tavern Tortilla Soup 109
   Waterfront Gumbo 116
   White Chili 105
   Winter Vegetable Soup 106
Sour Cream Drop Cookies 237
Southern Corn Pudding 196
Spareribs 76

Spectacular Platter 184
Spicy Chicken with Peanut Sauce ... 59
Spicy Marinated Shrimp 29
Spicy Tortilla Casserole 144
Spiked Apple Pie 250

Spinach
   Mandarin Blue Spinach Salad ... 215
   Spinach and Feta Pizza 150
Sterling Sugar Cookies 235

Strawberries
   Frozen Lime Torte
     with Blackberry Sauce
     and Fresh Fruit 246
   Strawberries Excellent 179
Stuffed Flank Steak 48
Summer Tomato Dressing 231
Summer Veggie Pasta Salad 225
Sun-Dried Tomato Spread 19

Sweet Potatoes
   Holiday Sweet Potatoes 198
   Sweet Potato Casserole 199
   Sweet Potato Rolls 164

T

Tailgate Brisket 52
Tangy Fruit Pork Chops 79
Tantalizing Pea Salad 227
Tarragon Chicken Salad 216
Tavern Tortilla Soup 109
Three-Cheese Ravioli 125
Tiramisu 245

Tomatoes
   Confetti Rice 212
   Creamy Tomato-Sausage
     Sauce with Shells 134
   Crostini with Toppers 12
   Cumin Chicken with
     Hot Citrus Salsa 60
   Eggplant-Tomato Casserole 191
   Fresh Tomato-Basil Casserole 194
   Hearty Chili 110
   Sassy Sausage Dip 22

What Can I Bring?

Summer Tomato Dressing 231
Sun-Dried Tomato Spread 19
Tomato and Basil Salad 228
Tomato and Onion Tart 169
Tomato Company Cups 21
Tomato Pie 190
Tomato-Basil Vinaigrette
   for Pasta 122
Tortilla-Black Bean Casserole 135

Turkey
Sausage and Roasted
   Vegetable Couscous 138
Spicy Tortilla Casserole 144
Tuxedo Cups 243

V

Veal Scaloppine 97
Vegetable Quiche 167
Vegetable Stir-Fry
   with Ginger Sauce 148
Veggie and Bean Quesadillas 140
Vidalia Onion and
   Rice Casserole 210
Vienna Breakfast Muffins 159
Virginia Bicentennial
   Chicken Salad 146
Virginia Country Ham Spread 23

W

Walnut Broccoli 183
Waterfront Gumbo 116
White and Dark Brownies 242
White Chili 105
White Lasagna 127
Winter Vegetable Soup 106

Y

Yogurt-Dill Sauce 87

Z

Zesty Herb Dressing 185
Zesty Stuffed Zucchini 195

Zucchini
Dark Zucchini Bread 157
Garden Fresh Frittata 168
Middleburg Medley 182
Oven-Roasted Vegetables 204
Spectacular Platter 184
Summer Veggie Pasta Salad 225
Veggie and Bean Quesadillas 140
Zesty Stuffed Zucchini 195
Zucchini Enchiladas 141

Contributors

Donna Adams
Cynthia Adler
Carole Allred
Erin Anderson-Quilici
Stephanie Andrejcak
Morrow Armstrong
Leann Asma
Ann Ault
Tracy Ault
Melissa Azzam
Susan Barclay*
Lorraine Bargess
Karen Barker
Ann M. Barrett
Jane Bateman
Camille Battaglia
Lou Baumgartner
Debbie Bayly
Candace Beane*
Elizabeth Biskaduros
Valerie Blatnik-Sigel
Nicole Boer*
Soley Boland
Kristin Bonacci
Eula Bond
Carol Bowen*
Katie Bradley*
Chris Bresett*
Arlene Buchman
Melissa Buckner
Maija K. Budow
Laura Bumpus
Lorraine Burgess
Kendra Burlingame
Virginia Burroughs
Candy Burt
Quincy Butler
Mary Cahill
Elizabeth Caldwell
Caren T. Camp
Tammy Cantow
Esther Capasse
Billie Cardwell
Barbara Carroll
Mary Beth Carroll*
Kathy Carter*
Ruth Carter
Kristin Collie
Kitty Collins
Carol Claybrook Colobro
Liz Conners
Karen Connolly
Lee Corey-Turner
Jackie Coston
Madeline Countess
Barbara Crandall*
Dale Croxton
Cindy Curtis
Genny Dairymple
J. Danker
Paige Dannenbaum
Mary Ellen Davis
Reba Davis
Jeanne Davison*
Sasha Day*
JoJo Dean
Beth DeWeerdt*
Leesa Jordan Dodd

Anne Donohue
Johanna Donovan
Amy Draper
Ann A. Duffey
Quang Duong
Judith Earp
Caroline Eberhardt
Claire Edwards
Ellen Ellis
June Evans
Jennifer Eversman
Liz Farnum
Rene Faulkner
Ann Felton
Jack Felton
Joanne Felton
Sarah Felton
Emily Fergus
Scarlett Ferguson
Jennifer Fincken
Jean Fisher
Mary Flack
Heather Flaherty*
Dina Flynn
Mary Flynn
Joni Foorter
Eleanor Forsythe
Jerry Fox
"Nana" Fox
Michelle France
Betsy Frantz*
Francie Freitas
Barbara Frisbie
Mary Fritz
Jan Johnston Fuchs
Heather Call Fuller
Savannah Fung
Susan Gaddy
Ann D. Gaffey*
Carol Gardiner
Mary Garner
Andy Gaylord
Catherine Giacomo
Stephanie Giorgis
Martha Girard
Jennifer Gladieux
Melissa Gonzalez
Lesley Goodrich
Lucy Gordon
Jennifer Grady
Kimberly Graf*
Elizabeth Graves
Katie Graves
Vicki Greve
Connie Goldsberry Griffin
Eric Grimes
Kathy Grimes
Elizabeth Groves*
Emily Gunn
Romy Gunter-Nathan
Lisa Harder
Lisa Hardin
Ann Fox Harrison
Gordon Harrison
Janet Hawkins
Alison Hawley
Erin Hawley
Kate Golden Hayes

Vicki Healy
Debbie Heck*
Jean Heck
Melissa Held
Mary Mouritsen Henderson
Stephanie Henke
Missy Henriksen
Jane S. Herde
Michael E. Herde
Nancy Jumper Herde*
Kristin Hermsmeyer
Julie Hershom
Claire Hines
Kathleen Hofer
Susan Hornyar
Heather Houston*
Lee Ann Howdershell
Kathy Huddleston
Mrs. Don Hunziker
Tricia Hutcherson
Kellye Jennings*
Sharon Johnsen*
Allison Johnson
Annelle Johnson*
Dee Johnson
Elizabeth Johnson
Helen Johnson
Hilda Johnson
Jane Johnson
Jennifer A. Johnson
Leigh Ann Johnston
Beth Jones
Jennifer Jones
Eda Joyce
Rosa America Jumper
Shari Petty Jumper
Julie Jumper-Morris
Janice Kaufman
Ellen Kay
Suzy Kazul
John Keane
Tracy Kennedy*
Dru Kevit
Neil King
Carla Klein
Joyce M. Klein
Louise Klein
Bonnie Klem
Margaret Klekner-Segretto
Jane N. Koch
Jennifer Koch
Mary Krueger*
Susan LaChance
Rene Ladd
Beth LaFollette
Shelia Landau
MK Lanzillotta
Linda Lathrop
Pam Laucella
Shelly Lawrence
Karen Lemke
Diane Lestina
Claudia Lewis
Jennifer Lewis
Connie Lindsley
Anne M. Link
Anne Lockhart
Marion Loras

Sharon Forsythe Luther
Jayne Talbot Lyons
Jennifer Mainardi
Dana Malloy
Lisa Maloney*
Anne Marquardt*
Cary Cox Martin
John Martin
Whitney Mason
Charlene Masse
Joyce Mattson
Beth McCartney
Malinda McCulloch*
Betty Sue McDonald
Donna McDonald
Pam Hunziker McDorman
Ruth Miller McElroy*
Charlotte McGlaughlin
Diane McGrath
Sallie McHugh
Anne Miniter McKay
Melissa McLallen
Kim McLeod
Meg McLeod
Ethel McMahon
Carolyn Meade
Carol Melim*
Laura Melnick
Marjory Melnick
Debby Melnikoff
Kendra Mendenhall
Lynn Reese Mendenhall*
Minda Mendoze
Molly Mengebier*
Jayne Merritt
Claire Messinger
Abby Meyer
Uffe Mikkelsen
Melinda Miller
June Million
Lilly Mondella
Joyce Montgomery
Carey Monts
Cheryl Moore
Jan Moore
Catherine Morris*
Jenifer Morris
Kris Morris
Rocky Morris
Ann Mosher
Dave Mosher
Charlene Mosse
Linda Mowry
Elizabeth Murphy
Eve Murty*
Liz Myers
Emily Naegeli*
Paige Nassetta
Mary Ann Neal*
Katherine Nesbit*
Sherri Nickles
Betsy Nolan*
Michelle L. Norwood
Anne Lee Nottingham
Fran Nugent*
Lisa Nugent
Lisa O'Donnell
Leva K. O'Rourke
Lynette Olifer
Nancy Olson
Fran Orr

Jennifer Papandon
Dolores Parker
Glenda Parsons
Kimberly Person
Cynthia (CJ) Peters*
Ruth Peters
Lynn Phillips
Carolyn Phipps
Claudia Pleasants
Mike Pool
Peggy Pool*
Diane Post
Mike Post
Diane Powell*
Virginia Price
Christine Quigley
Lynn Quillin*
Ann Railsback
Audrey Rajchel
Anne Clark Ramsay
Beth Redmond
Sandy Reilly
Mandy Reynolds*
Louise Rhoads
Valerie Hunziker Richardson*
Frances Robinson
Kelly Rodenburg
Emily Romanchuk
Sarah Rothleder
Janice Ann Rowe
Annie Jewel Royle
Linda Rudd
Shelley Sabo*
Gladys Sandlin
Kim Sanz
Terri Sarfan
Mary Schoen
Fran Scofield
Elizabeth Scott
Katherine Scott
Kathleen Scott
Marilou Serafin
Kay Serea
Betty Seybold
Laura Seybold
MariAnn Seybold*
Valerie Shank
Marcia Sherwin
Katharine Sieminski*
Erin Sievers
Molly Sim
Sherry Sites
Cynthia Smerdzinski
Richard Smoot
Kathy Spong
Kim Stackman
Beth Stallsworth*
Mary Margaret Stevens
Claire Stitt
Elaine Stottlemyer
AnnMarie Strabo
Ashley Strand
Laura Swanstrom
Mary Lou Swartz
Christy Sweet
Suzanne Sylvester
Jan Symons
Debbie Talley
Susan Taylor
Mary Teale
Laura Thomasch

Mary Bea Thurston
Christina Torgesen
Jill Townsend-Zulik
Florence D. Trigg
Ed Tyszka
Connie van Zandt
Jo Villemarette*
Melissa Viscovich
Christina Volzer*
Laura Vordewhiele
Jamie Vroom
Mrs. Nicholas Vurdelja
Jennifer C. Walsh
Susan Warren
Elizabeth Wash
Crystal Waters
Joyce Weaber*
Mollie Weber
Pamela Fox Weber
Ellen Webster*
Terry Weipert
Casey Cashion Weiser*
Penny Wenzell
Matt Werner
Terri Werner*
Debbie Whelan
Lyndy Whipp
Debi Whitaker
Kristine Wichin
Patricia Willingham
Helen Ann Willmott
Lisa R. Wilson
Jean Withers
Pamela Wiley Wood
Rhonda Wydeven
Kate Wyckoff
Liz Yancey
Nicole Young
Willie Young
Sally Yuen
Jill Zimmerman
Mary Zinsner*
Micaela Zirkle VMD*
Suzanne Zolldan*

Acknowledgments

Alexandria Convention &
Visitors Association

Amano

Corso de'Fion

Ford's Theater

Francie Freitas

Great Falls Park, National Park
Service

Gunston Hall Plantation

Meadowlark Gardens,
Northern Virginia Regional
Park Authority

Michael Round

Mount Vernon Estate and
Gardens

Mr. and Mrs. Bob Cooney

Kay Sierra

The John F. Kennedy Center for
the Performing Arts

"What Can I Bring?"

Thank you for supporting the purpose and community
programs of the Junior League of Northern Virginia, Inc.

Please send me _____ copies   @ $19.95 each _____

Virginia residents add 4.5% sales tax   @ $ .90 each _____

Postage & handling $ 5.00 each _____

Postage and handling for
  each additional book to the same address   @ $ 2.00 each _____

                                             Total _____

Name: _____

Address: _____

City: _____ State: _____ Zip: _____

❏ Check or money order enclosed. Make check payable to JLNV.

❏ Visa/MasterCard# _____ Exp: _____

Signature: _____

Mail to: PO Box 9980, McLean, VA 22102

Phone: (703) 893-0258 Fax: (703) 734-8964

"What Can I Bring?"

Thank you for supporting the purpose and community
programs of the Junior League of Northern Virginia, Inc.

Please send me _____ copies   @ $19.95 each _____

Virginia residents add 4.5% sales tax   @ $ .90 each _____

Postage & handling $ 5.00 each _____

Postage and handling for
  each additional book to the same address   @ $ 2.00 each _____

                                             Total _____

Name: _____

Address: _____

City: _____ State: _____ Zip: _____

❏ Check or money order enclosed. Make check payable to JLNV.

❏ Visa/MasterCard# _____ Exp: _____

Signature: _____

Mail to: PO Box 9980, McLean, VA 22102

Phone: (703) 893-0258 Fax: (703) 734-8964